MODERN MINDFULNESS

How to Be More Relaxed, Focused,
and Kind While Living in a Fast,
Digital, Always-On World

ROHAN GUNATILLAKE

bluebird
books for life

First published as *This Is Happening* in 2016 by Bluebird
This paperback edition published 2017 by Bluebird
an imprint of Pan Macmillan
20 New Wharf Road, London N1 9RR
Associated companies throughout the world
www.panmacmillan.com

ISBN 978-1-5098-4863-8

The author would like to thank the following for the use of their icons
in chapters 2–7: Molly Bramlet, Richard de Vos, Blake Kathryn, Nikita
Kozin, Nicholas Menghini, Stefan Parnarov, Lukasz Pogoda, Danny
Sturgess, Alex Tai, Jens Tärning, Aha-Soft and Creative Stall.

1 3 5 7 9 8 6 4 2

A CIP catalogue record for this book is available from the British Library.

Typeset by Richard Marston, www.richardmarston.com
Printed and bound by CPI Group (UK) Ltd, Croydon, CR0 4YY

Visit **www.panmacmillan.com** to read more about all our books
and to buy them. You will also find features, author interviews and
news of any author events, and you can sign up for e-newsletters
so that you're always first to hear about our new releases.

To my parents and yours

Contents

Chapter 1

A Very Modern Mindfulness

Mindfulness needs a redesign.

There has never been as much interest in mindfulness and meditation as there is right now. A growing base of scientific research is providing substantial evidence for its benefits and effects. Leading companies are teaching it to their employees to manage stress. Elite athletes use it to stay calm and perform under pressure. Celebrities are taking it on as a must-have lifestyle accessory, and most importantly, people just like you are discovering how making mindfulness part of their lives can have a significantly positive impact. That's the good news.

The bad news is that despite all this, most people who have an interest in mindfulness do not actually go on to do anything about it. There are three main barriers that stop people moving mindfulness from a nice idea to a lived reality: the time problem, the hippy problem and the digital problem. As a maker of mindfulness-related products, these are actually the challenges that get me the most excited since they can all be overcome.

I just don't have time to meditate. This is the time problem. In an over-scheduled world with all our various commitments, finding a quiet ten or twenty minutes to dedicate to ourselves feels like an impossible task. So when we hear that to get the most out of mindfulness we have to do exactly that, of course it feels out of reach. If this is you, please don't worry. We'll solve the time problem.

You have to be spiritual or religious to get into meditation and that's just not me. This is the hippy problem. Mindfulness-based meditation does originate from the Buddhist tradition. And even though Buddhism has perhaps the best PR department out of all the major world religions, the spiritual aesthetic and other baggage tied up with mindfulness and meditation is a very real barrier for a lot of people. That's fine too. We will solve the hippy problem.

I live a very connected life and it's just not practical for me to unplug everything. This is the digital problem. Mindfulness and technology are commonly presented as being in opposition to each other. Too often we are told that the only way to be truly present and connected is to turn everything off. But in a world where our work, our lifestyle and our economy are so fundamentally dependent on technology, when it comes to our wellbeing we simply cannot afford to keep demonising all things digital. But fear not. We will solve the digital problem as well.

This is a next-generation mindfulness book. It is for the millions of people who struggle to find space in the busyness of it all. It is for the millions of people all around the world who would love more awareness, more calm and more kindness in their lives. It is for the millions of people who have never felt that mindfulness or meditation was for them. This book is for you.

Notice what it feels like to read these opening paragraphs. Notice if any particularly strong thoughts or reactions have come up. Maybe there's some excitement. Maybe there's some doubt.

Notice if there are any clear physical sensations present in the body. Maybe you can notice what your breath is like right now. Or what the movements that make up blinking actually feel like. Or even the simple sensations you can feel from holding this book in your hands. This is going to be fun. This is happening.

———

If you *are* the kind of person who can easily find time in your day for formal sitting meditation practice, don't have a problem with bald people in robes telling you what to do, and can give up using your digital devices, then congratulations. There are already plenty of good mindfulness and meditation approaches out there that will work for you. But the chances are that you're not. The three problems I mentioned previously are often thought of as just being facts of meditation life. *That's what mindfulness is like, deal with it.* This is just plain wrong and the reason why we need a mindfulness that is better designed for the realities of our modern lives.

The approach outlined in this book solves the time problem by reframing meditation primarily as a mobile activity – something we can do everywhere, not just when sitting on a cushion in a quiet space. It solves the hippy problem by understanding that while it certainly has religious roots, mindfulness has evolved and is now being used for reasons that are entirely new. It solves the digital problem by embracing the importance of technology in our lives and learning how to actually use our devices as the *basis* of our wellbeing, not its nemesis.

The alternative is that we simply carry on thinking about mindfulness in the same ways that we do today. If we do, then mindfulness will continue to be a minority sport. It will be a luxury, unavailable to the vast majority of people whose lifestyles and values do not fit with the conventional presentation. Given the growing evidence of how mindfulness practice can lead to so many different positive outcomes, that would be a real shame. *Here is this awesome thing but, sorry, it's not for you.*

As well as being a shame, it would be ignoring the fact that the story of mindfulness is one of innovation and change. Later on we'll look more closely at how mindfulness has evolved over time and also where it might go next. However, before starting out in our adventures into mindfulness, there is one big idea that it is worth you knowing. Mindfulness is a flexible tradition and it has a long history of reimagining itself every time it meets a new culture. The ways in which mindfulness is changing today are therefore just a natural next chapter as it adapts in response to things it has only recently met, such as neuroscience, psychology and digital technology.

Referring to the history of mindfulness and how it

changes doesn't need to feel abstract. What we are actually talking about are individuals like you and me taking what has gone before and working out how best to apply that to the realities of our lives as they are right now. My own big breakthrough was when I discovered how to meditate in a time-poor world. It not only changed my understanding of mindfulness, it went on to change my whole life.

Finding the future of mindfulness on the way to work

I got into meditation during my last few months at university and upon graduation I moved back to London to begin work with a large technology consulting company. It was an exciting time all round. I was enjoying the energetic corporate lifestyle, making decent headway into my student debt, and my interest in mindfulness and meditation was really starting to take off. I had begun to look for classes and groups near me, and I was even considering going on a weekend retreat.

The problem was that I didn't have time to fit it all in. I'd had no such problems in my student life, where I could happily find a spare half hour. But it was entirely different now that I had been fast-tracked into the long-work-hours corporate culture. Even when I did find time for dedicated sitting meditation, I was often so tired that the quality of my attention and energy was such that I could not do it justice. So I was surprised when I found the solution to my problem on the Northern Line one Monday morning.

While all the routes of the London Underground have their challenges, the Northern Line is probably the most soul-destroying. And it is in the mornings that it is at its worst. Cities get a bad rap as lonely, disconnecting places at the best of times, but it's perhaps most clearly felt when travelling deep underground in a confined space, surrounded by strangers but very much alone. Most mornings on my half-hour ride from south London into the City, what I most clearly felt was the shoulder of another anonymous worker squashed expertly into my unsuspecting face.

On top of the normal frustrations of commuting, I was now particularly resentful of the Northern Line because it was taking away from my meditation time. Mornings were my favourite time to do sitting meditation. Not only was there the freshness of the recently woken-up mind, but mornings also provided me with a reliable sense of routine since I often had to work late and so didn't know what time I would be home. The problem now was that I was on a project that consistently required me to be in the office very early, and I just didn't have any time to do my sitting.

By some miracle that morning I had been able to snag a seat. So there I sat, wallowing in the woe-is-me story about losing my favourite time to meditate. The mind does love snowballing a tiny thought into a giant catastrophe, so I was of course also convinced that my job, which I loved, meant I would never be able to meditate properly again. It was all over.

The style of meditation I was doing at the time was one which is very commonly taught to people starting out. You pay attention to the physical sensations of the breath, and whenever your attention gets distracted, you just bring it back, developing both awareness and stability. The problem I now had while doing that on the Underground was that even with my eyes closed, there were just so many other physical sensations going on. All the shaking, noise, heat and constant bumping into my fellow passengers meant that I was not able to even find the breath at all, let alone stick with it. Frustration ran riot. *I'm useless. The Tube is useless. Everything. Is. Useless.*

It was in the middle of this self-pitying funk that the cartoon light bulb popped above my head. Since I was on the Tube at the same time of day that I used to do meditation at home, why not just do my meditation on the Tube instead? The journey was the same length as my normal meditation, and I was also sitting down. Who cares that the circumstances were a little unusual for meditation? Inspired by that insight, the next twenty or so minutes went on to completely change my understanding of what it is to meditate.

Just like that, the frustration disappeared. My realisation that I could meditate anywhere if I really wanted to has underpinned my approach to mindfulness ever since. When keeping the mind on the breath, it is the mind – and our ability to keep our awareness present and in one place – that is the important thing, not the breath. When that became clear, I stopped worrying about holding my attention on the breath and was just aware of whatever was most tangible at the time. I became aware of what it was to sit in that moment. I felt the vibrations of the carriage and discovered angles and sensations I hadn't noticed before. I felt the way that my muscles reacted to how we were accelerating and decelerating. By taking care of *how* I was being aware rather than *what* I was being aware of, there was a natural level of non-distraction.

I then opened my attention out and began listening to the sounds around me. With my mind open and relaxed I noticed how the various sounds came into my awareness without me having to do anything, just as they did when I would do my more conventional formal meditation. Opening my eyes and looking at my fellow passengers, I even noticed that there was a quiet sense of gratitude. I recognised it as the same feeling I had at the end of a group meditation class – because, although they may not have meant to, they had played their part.

My understanding of meditation had changed forever.

Defining the M word

There is often a lot of confusion about what mindfulness and meditation actually are. Are they the same thing? Are they different? Are they both the same and different? Oh dear.

The two words are used in various and entangled ways in all sorts of contexts, even in such respected places as clinical research papers. No wonder it is confusing. As someone involved in the presentation of the stuff, I do have to take some responsibility. So let's clear it up once and for all.

Of the two, meditation is the easiest to define. Meditation is the use of techniques to direct our attention in order to help train us in positive qualities such as concentration, clarity of awareness and acceptance. There are many different mental qualities that can be trained. There are also many different techniques by which to train a single quality. Meditation can be done in a very formal way, such as in the classic sitting posture with eyes closed for a dedicated period of time. Or it can be done in a more dynamic, mobile style alongside our everyday activities, as will be emphasised in this book. All of which means that meditation is an overarching umbrella term which covers a universe of techniques from all kinds of traditions and used for all kinds of outcomes.

Mindfulness is a touch more difficult to define. The technical definition of mindfulness is knowing what is happening in our experience while it is happening. It is the reason that this book is called what it is. When we are aware of what is happening in our experience at any one time, be it physical sensations in our body or thoughts or emotions in our mind, then there is mindfulness. The quality of mindfulness is an absolutely central part of meditation, especially in what is known as insight meditation, which is the particular style from which the modern mindfulness movement largely derives.

The reason that definitions have become a little bit confusing is that there was a point at which using the word meditation became very unfashionable. Meditation first came into public consciousness during the sixties and seventies. Members of the so-called 'hippy' generation became

Ultimately, whether we call it mindfulness, meditation or anything else, what we are talking about is the deliberate and active use of our mind to improve our mind.

enamoured with the romantic spiritual traditions of Asia and brought what they had learnt back home once their visas and money finally ran out. Ever since then we have suffered from what I call the 'hippy hangover'.

Meditation began as a primarily spiritual practice. That has changed in the last forty years. Meditation, and in particular mindfulness-based meditation, is now being used in a whole range of very different contexts, from the workplace to dealing with clinical mental health conditions. Despite meditation having moved on from its spiritual roots, the perception of meditation as being something that was still very much the domain of the alternative scene proved hard to budge. People therefore found that it was much easier to get funding for medical research and sign-off for training programmes from multinational companies when they talked about mindfulness rather than meditation. And it sort of stuck.

In this book I will use the words meditation and mindfulness interchangeably since that is the most common way they are used today. There are many different technical definitions for mindfulness but I think those are best saved for the more academic literature. Ultimately, whether we call it mindfulness, meditation or anything else, what we are talking about is the deliberate and active use of our mind to improve our mind. That's really all we need to know.

———

I have been practising and studying mindfulness for more than twelve years. In the last few years I have also gone on to make mindfulness-based apps and products. My personal and professional adventures have shown me that there is an exciting new mindfulness game in town and that game has new rules. We've already met the first of them on that fateful commute into work on the Northern Line.

Rule #1:
Make mindfulness first and foremost a mobile activity

People who say they don't have time for mindfulness or meditation are not necessarily wrong. But they are not seeing the whole picture. The key is understanding the difference between formal and informal practice.

Formal practice is the most common idea of what meditation is. It is what happens when we sit down in a quiet place, close our eyes and dedicate a period of time to our technique of choice. Whenever meditation is presented in pop culture this is what it looks like. Someone sitting cross-legged, often with their fingers in the OK-sign, hands balanced on their knees. There may even be an 'om' or two thrown in for good measure.

Formal practice is incredibly important. It allows us to deepen the quality of our mindfulness, encourages a sense of complete stillness and can result in insights that can really support us throughout our life. However, to get the most out of formal practice we need to dedicate quiet time for it, and you may well have noticed that time is an increasingly scarce resource in our modern world. What price a spare quiet hour on a weekday afternoon with no distractions?

In response to this so-called 'time poverty', we find formal meditation being presented in a way that constantly reduces the time commitment required. *Twenty minutes of meditation is all you need. No, actually scratch that, ten minutes of meditation is all you need. If you don't have time for ten minutes, that's OK, here's a power-packed five-minute meditation you can use.* There are even apps for one-minute meditations. And even shorter still.

While it absolutely is possible to carve out time for formal meditation practice when we really want to, it is just a fact of twenty-first-century life that most of us struggle to find quality quiet time. If this was the whole picture, then that would be incredibly bad news for mindfulness because despite all its well-documented benefits, the one resource needed to make it happen is harder and harder to find. This is where informal practice comes to our rescue.

Informal meditation practice is what happens when we make the decision to use any activity we happen to be engaged in as the basis for our development of awareness, calm or kindness. It is a mobile and real-time style of meditation for a mobile and real-time world. It is also very effective.

All we need is a basic understanding of core meditation techniques, and the will, energy and confidence to make them part of our everyday life. This is what this book will give you.

Some of us are fortunate enough to clock up eight hours of sleep every night. We may also be virtuous enough to do ten, twenty or even thirty minutes of sitting practice every day. That still leaves the best part of sixteen hours which we're effectively writing off from a mindfulness perspective, aside from hoping that the effects of our formal practice somehow leak through into the rest of our day. This is why informal practice is so important. It uses the time we already have rather than asking us to create some more time that we can't.

However, the danger of calling one style of meditation formal and the other informal is that it can make us think that formal is more important. This distinction is a mistake and is the number one reason people subscribe to the time problem. Both informal and formal practice are as important as each other. My argument is that since the time we have for informal practice is perhaps fifty to a hundred times more than what we have for formal practice, it should become our priority. So rather than call it informal meditation, we will call it mobile meditation or mobile mindfulness. You could also call it on-the-go meditation or out-and-about meditation.

Both formal and mobile practice have been part of the mindfulness tradition since the very beginning. In fact, the distinction between the two was never originally made and the cultivation of qualities such as stability, curiosity and compassion were encouraged at all times and in all situations. As the various meditation traditions developed and evolved over the centuries, they each gave different levels of emphasis to mobile practice, with some making it their primary style. The overall idea of mobile mindfulness, therefore, is neither new nor my own invention. It is, however, one whose time has arrived for a comeback.

Formal meditation is often considered as having trickle-down effects. It is said that if we do formal practice then the benefits of that will somehow transfer to the rest of our life. That may well be the case but given that the rest of our life is so much bigger, this book will turn the whole idea of prioritising formal meditation on its head. It will present a picture in which we primarily train our mindfulness alongside our everyday activities. We will still use formal practice, but it will be in a secondary role as a way to support and deepen the benefits rather than as the main event. As a result, we no longer have the excuse of not having time. The main problem then becomes knowing what techniques to use and remembering to use them. And those problems are much easier to solve than making time in an already too full schedule.

This change, from formal to mobile, is one you will already be very familiar with from personal computing. If you are at least twenty years old, like me you'll remember a time when if you wanted to work, play games or check your inbox, you had to go to a specific room in your house and sit down in front of a large beige box. Today we have all that power and more in our phones and tablets, which we can use wherever we happen to be. We still use desktop computers for the things that we can't quite do on our phones, but we now live in a mobile-first world.

It's time for mindfulness and meditation to move there too.

Incense sticks not required

I never thought that I would end up making a living from creating things which helped bring mindfulness to so many people. One of the real pleasures of making mindfulness stuff is that I get the chance to engage with people who have found it useful in their lives and are moved enough to share their stories with me. Jennifer is one of those people who recently got in touch with me. She is an ambitious lawyer with a young son and the story she shared with me is one I have heard all too often.

There are two main reasons why people get into meditation: crisis or curiosity. If you're like me and came in through curiosity, then you will mainly be motivated by an interest in how your mind works. You have an inkling of how big an impact your inner life – your thoughts and emotions – has on you and the people around you. You have a sense, however small, that taking care of that inner life is fundamental to your wellbeing. So you turn to mindfulness as a way to support that.

Curiosity, however, is the much less common of the two entry points. For most people it is crisis which sends them knocking on the mindfulness door. People come in via crisis because they have had one or more truly difficult experiences in their lives and are looking for anything that might help them out. Crisis comes in a range of flavours. It can sometimes look like a condition such as depression, anxiety or chronic pain. Or it can look like something much less clinical but just as powerful such as work stress, the inability to sleep or the end of a relationship. Or it can simply be the feeling that we just can't cope.

It was this sense of not being able to cope that led Jennifer to try meditation. When we spoke she told me that she felt she was drowning under the pressures of work, home and family. *I was losing myself in the storm and I wasn't sure if I could take any more. Something had to change.*

Jennifer had heard of how effective mindfulness can be in managing stress and so signed up to the only available class near her. She called in a favour from her mother to help manage childcare so she could make the sessions after work and was really excited to attend that first class. Finally she was going to get some support and learn how to develop the skills to deal with it all.

It was heartbreaking when I heard what actually happened. Jennifer hit the hippy problem and she hit it hard. It had started pretty well. The class began with a simple guided meditation all about paying attention to one's breath. And while she didn't find it easy or straightforward, given all the different thoughts and distractions which came up during that short period, she got the sense that there was something to this meditation thing.

Then it all started unravelling. Despite being billed as a

secular class, the teacher began to introduce things which were explicitly religious. There were statues, incense sticks and ritual bells. There was even chanting. Jennifer squirmed her way through the rest of the evening, left before the tea and biscuits and never went back. She was attracted to the promise of meditation but her upbringing, personal history and values meant she was full-on averse to anything outwardly religious. It was just too high a barrier for her to overcome. *If this is what meditation is, then it's not for me.* So she turned her back on mindfulness and just muddled through, not giving it another thought. Then she had her second child two years later and, while she loved being a mother, the day-to-day logistics of life became even more of a struggle. She remembered her original interest in mindfulness and, even though she was scarred by her first experience, she decided to give it another go. This time she started with an app she'd been recommended by a friend and that is how she ended up getting in touch with me. She had finally found a way in where she didn't need to take on any spiritual baggage and the lowering of that barrier meant she could start making mindfulness real and enjoy all the benefits that come with that.

Unfortunately, this is a common experience. It takes a lot of bravery to go to a meditation class for the first time. We are recognising that maybe we don't have all the answers right now and could do with some skills and support to get through. That means we have to show some vulnerability and that takes real courage. That's why I find stories such as Jennifer's so heartbreaking. Due to a bad first experience, many people are so put off that despite an urgent desire to deal with their difficulties and face their inner lives, they end up not doing anything about it for years. Some people even have such a negative experience that they are put off for life.

Nowadays, thankfully, there are many different ways into mindfulness that do not require you to subscribe to a spiritual or religious point of view. However, the hippy hangover still runs deep. Meditation is still popularly perceived primarily as a spiritual practice that is limited to something you do on a cushion. The truth is that it is much more than that and always has been. Understanding that is the second rule of mobile mindfulness.

Rule #2:
Mindfulness should be led by what people want, not by tradition

There was a time in the history of mindfulness when the only way to get into it was through religion and spirituality. That has now changed. The spiritual motivation for meditating does exist and is still an important part of the picture but it is now only one part, not the whole kahuna. Nowadays people have completely different motivations for getting into mindfulness. Workplace stress, medical conditions, performance under high pressure and the everyday ability to deal with everyday difficulties are just some of them.

The mistake made most often is to bring out the holy steamroller and start from a spiritual or religious position irrespective of what people are actually interested in using mindfulness for. So what typically happens is that a style of meditation that has worked well for a spiritual motivation is adjusted to fit a newer, different motivation. The problem with this approach is that certain ingredients of how meditation has been presented for spiritual reasons – the language, the aesthetic, the ritual elements, the methods of practice – are so baked into that presentation that they are not remotely in scope for change, even though they can put off a significant proportion of the potential audience. *Well, that's just how meditation is, so if you don't like it, then it's nothing to do with the way we're presenting it, it's just that you're wrong.*

This is where good design comes in. If people don't want the religious wrapping paper but still want the gift of mindfulness, then the obvious solution is to switch things up. What we need to do is wrap the gift the way that is most likely for someone to want to open it and make sure the gift is what the receiver actually wants. *I know you wanted a bike for Christmas but here's a Buddha statue instead.*

So the second new rule of mobile mindfulness is all about starting with where you are and letting meditation meet you there instead of you having to go out and change before you can even get through the door. If your most pressing need is to calm down in stressful situations, then you should be able to access that part of mindfulness right away. If you are struggling with difficult experience such as anxiety or other emotional issues, you should be able to get support aimed specifically at that. And it should all be presented in such a way that feels natural to the realities and aesthetics of your life here and now. This seemingly obvious idea is why this book is structured like it is.

The journey from mind-full to mindful

If you've ever used your phone or another device to track your sleep, calorie intake, steps or even your heartbeat, then whether you know it or not, you have been part of the so-called 'Quantified Self movement'. This geeky term is what's used to talk about anyone who uses technology to track and analyse information about the details of their personal life. The idea behind it is that tracking all this information is a positive force that allows us to make better decisions about how we live our lives.

Tennessee-based Chris Dancy is a leading figure in the Quantified Self movement. Once labelled by the press as the most connected human on the planet, Chris is an extreme tracker. He has set up systems that can track tens of thousands of different data points across all parts of his life and at any one time will actively monitor and analyse over fifteen hundred. And you think *you* suffer from information overload?

Soon after starting his personal regime of full-scale tracking, Chris began to notice real benefits from being aware of all that he was doing. Seeing the connections between what he did and how he felt had helped him lose a significant amount of weight as well as improve how he managed his moods. But three years in, it started to get a bit too much. *Googling your name is just about* OK. *But when you can google your entire life, it becomes overwhelming. I don't think you're supposed to browse your life. You're not supposed to be able to bookmark your emotions*. It even got to the point where just by looking at his data, he could predict when he was going to feel depressed. It was too much. But he didn't stop tracking. Instead he turned to mindfulness.

It's the stillness. In a digital world, being still is often perceived as a problem, that something is broken. But it's stillness that we need to be human. We need the gaps. We've created all this technology but instead of it helping us become more human, we are in danger of becoming too much in its service.

When practised consistently, mindfulness gives us the clarity required to see the connections between things. All the technology that Chris engages with on a moment-by-moment basis gives him information he can then analyse over time, and with that longer view make changes in his life for the better. But without the stability he is able to develop through his meditation practice, Chris says he could not necessarily have all the inner resources to deal with his information-laden life. He now considers the integration of technology into his life as so natural that he describes himself as a mindful cyborg.

While Chris is perhaps on the extreme end of things, his number one piece of advice to those of us looking for a more balanced digital life is relevant to everyone: avoid digital dualism. Coined by Nathan Jurgenson, 'digital dualism' is a term used to talk about the separation we make between the online and the offline, between the so-called virtual and the so-called real. *But there's just life. When we create this dualistic view, we place the human in conflict with the machine, when actually it should always be just about being more whole.*

I agree. The act of drawing a line between the online and the offline, the digital world and the 'real world', is highly

The act of drawing a line between the online and the offline, the digital world and the 'real world', is highly problematic.

problematic. Firstly, it is not what our lives are actually like. As soon as we put a smartphone in our pocket, the division between online and offline disappears. This distinction is now increasingly redundant as more and more objects, from cars to fridges to trainers, become connected to the internet.

There is, however, a more dangerous consequence of perpetuating digital dualism – conflict. If my meditation has taught me anything over all these years, it is that whenever we draw a line and separate one thing from another, we are also creating conflict. Just the language of calling one thing 'virtual' and the other thing 'real' creates an enormous value judgement. Millions of people around the world find meaning from social interaction through digital channels. Is it fair to tell them that it is not real, not genuine? I don't think so. Thankfully this problem will be solved by time, in that there are still a significant proportion of us for whom this digital thing is entirely alien and therefore a threat. That will change.

This is a book that understands the dangers of digital dualism. So while digital technology is very much a major theme throughout, it is presented as just being a part of modern life rather than a special thing in itself. The theme of dealing with various aspects of our connected lives runs all through the book. It would be a mistake for a mobile mindfulness book to treat our digital lives as a special thing deserving of its own section or chapter since that would just be making yet another division and we've already got enough of those.

Speaking to Chris Dancy got me excited about how we can take more control over what benefits we get from all the technology that we engage with on a daily basis. His message is that we all have a big opportunity to use information and technology in service of our wellbeing so that it actually starts to nurture us as people. Chris calls this trend of technology transitioning from being an alien force to a nurturing one as moving from Big Brother to Big Mother. And that leads us to the third new rule of mindfulness.

Rule #3:
Make technology part of the solution, not the problem

All a meditation teacher can do is teach what they know. Part of the reason that mindfulness and technology are so often considered as being the opposite of each other is that the great generation of teachers who brought mindfulness to the West, and therefore catalysed its rapid development to where it is today, didn't grow up digital. Now that our most influential senior mindfulness teachers and experts are in their fifties and sixties, they are of a generation which are on the whole late adopters of our otherwise mainstream digital culture, if indeed they adopt it at all. This is exacerbated by the fact that many of them were part of the hippy movement, which while not anti-technology was at least suspicious of it.

It is therefore no surprise that since mindfulness has been transmitted to us through this generation of teachers, the technologies that have arisen as part of the digital revolution of the last fifteen years are often framed as the enemy, something against the natural order of things. To even say 'technology' in general indicates how crude the sentiment can be, for we're of course not talking about technologies such as traffic control systems or supermarket supply chain software. When technology is criticised in the context of modern behaviour we are mainly talking about personal, mobile, networked computing. That has led to a popular school of thought that the best way to deal with our perceived sense of information overload is to escape. We have to turn our phones off to be mindful. We observe a digital sabbath where all our devices are put away for a day a week. We may even spend a dedicated digital detox weekend that is as hipster as it is hippy, sewing and crafting in the woods, connecting with others, our phones checked in at the door.

All of these practices are good. There is enormous value in periods of abstinence. They allow us to take different perspectives and engage in activities that we otherwise may not have the time or space for. But by no means are they the whole answer.

I intensely dislike the term digital detox because it effectively says that our digital technologies are toxic. Those same technologies underpin our economy and our way of life and therefore, either as individuals or as a society, we are going to have a very hard time indeed if we continue to pathologise them. It is a highly unsustainable solution.

The idea of the retreat is historically very important to the mindfulness tradition. So when dealing with the challenges of digital life, the escape, the unplug and the detox are naturally the most commonly taught strategy. But while it is lovely to go on holiday, we can't be on holiday all the time. What is more, have you ever noticed that when your phone is off, it is not actually off? Because even then we know that emails are coming into our inbox, friends are posting messages that we're missing out on and major news is happening. For many of us this creates at best a sense of low-level anxiety. We live in an always-on world in which there is no off switch. Silent mode is not silent.

The opportunity that mobile mindfulness presents is to move past the binary thinking that our digital technology is either on or off, or that it's either a force for good or all that is wrong with the world. The opportunity is to change our relationship with our digital lives entirely. To use the power of technology to power our inner lives. In the last ten years we have seen popular technologies become normalised as a way to support our physical wellbeing. From the Nintendo Wii to the Apple Watch via workout apps and activity trackers, millions of people around the world already relate to their devices in a very positive way when it comes to fitness and physical health. The next step and the invitation of this book is to bring together mindfulness and modern life, thereby enabling the same to happen to our mental wellbeing, our mental health and our inner lives.

The alternative to not changing our relationship with technology fills me with dread. It points to our living in a society trapped in a dysfunctional relationship with the technologies on which it depends. No one wants that and it doesn't have to be that way.

Technology can definitely have a negative impact on our minds. Most money made on the web today is through advertising, and fortunes are made from the manipulation of our attention. As a result our minds have become fragmented and our distraction has become a habit. But no matter how large a supertanker is, it can be moved around. Throughout its history, meditation has always been used for breaking unhelpful habits and utilising the difficult stuff of life as the training ground for us to become better people.

It may feel that our digital lives are so overwhelming that we will just continue to get washed along with it all. But with the right intention, the right skills and a bit of effort we can go against the stream to get where we need to go. We can turn that tanker around. And what makes it all possible is the encouraging news that mindfulness and technology are not only natural partners, they could even be best friends. Because when you look more closely, they actually already are.

Where mindfulness and technology meet

It's a bright February morning in San Francisco and I am having a late breakfast. The cafe is full of young men and women huddled around shiny laptops. I overhear one group who are working on a presentation that they are pitching to investors later that week. There are two people sitting by the window, both of whom are writing code for their individual projects. This is a city obsessed by start-ups and everyone here seems to be working on what they hope will be the next Uber or Instagram.

The next time I look up from my toast and coffee I see one of the coders has put down his work and is clearly meditating. His back is upright, his shoulders are open, his eyes are closed and his hands are in a tell-tale position in his lap most commonly used in the Zen tradition. Ten or so minutes later he reopens his eyes, orders a muffin and goes back to work. No one bats an eyelid.

While more and more places around the world are becoming significant centres for start-ups and the technology world in general, San Francisco and the surrounding region, known as Silicon Valley, remains the global epicentre. And it is a place which is as much hippy as it is techie.

The most well-known meeting of contemplative practice and technology is in the influence that Zen Buddhism had on Steve Jobs, which led in part to the aesthetic and design principles for which Apple is so well known. This was, however, part of an ongoing story which came about thanks to a generation of leading technology practitioners and thinkers in the late sixties and seventies such as Stewart Brand and Kevin Kelly who, at the same time as laying the foundations for what we know as the digital world, were also exploring Asian culture and the then exotic practices of meditation.

In the intervening years, parts of that counterculture have become mainstream and some have remained at the margins. For several years the relationship between people pioneering outer technologies and those practising inner ones was not obvious. But today, mindfulness and meditation are back in a big way in and around Silicon Valley with many of its household-name companies and smaller start-ups running mindfulness courses for employees. San Francisco, Silicon Valley and California in general have a massive influence on today's globalised world. Much of what we now consider normal started as small-scale ideas in San Francisco garages, offices and cafes. Modern mindfulness will be no different.

The quickest way to recognise the relationship between meditation and technology is to see how meditation is itself a technology. You may have noticed that in the previous paragraph I snuck in the idea of meditation as an 'inner technology' and so I should explain that a little more. If technology is a set of tools and methods employed to solve certain problems or achieve certain objectives, then meditation is absolutely that. The key distinction is that meditation is working on primarily inner objectives rather than those on the outside.

It isn't hard to see that the general world of outer technology is accelerating away. We see rapid change everywhere we look. There are more mobile phones on the planet today than there are human beings. Apps and other software allow us to perform tasks that just a few years ago were the domain of technical specialists. Developments in medicine, home entertainment and transport point to a not-too-distant future where both lifestyle and lifespan may be very different to what we recognise as normal today.

Now what of our inner technologies? What are we doing to make sure that our inner worlds are developing in a similarly forward-facing trajectory? Even if we can't move at the exact same pace, can we use the tools and methods available to us to at least deal with this rapidly changing world?

Mindfulness-based meditation is one of those tools. It may not tune us up to the extent where we can take on the machines in tests of pure computational power, but it will help us develop the self-awareness, patience and openness that allow us to avoid becoming overwhelmed and to be more human. It all comes down to attention.

We live in an attention economy. You should have noticed that by now. Our attention is a valuable thing. Some companies make money directly from it. Others spend loads of money trying to get it from you. There are whole industries built around it. We live in a world dominated by advertising. Both on our screens and on our streets, our attention is bombarded and seduced in the hope that it will convert into a purchase. Our attention is a precious commodity. In a society where information is now effectively infinite and abundant, it is our attention that becomes the scarcest resource. The irony is that while the multinational companies all understand how valuable our attention is, we – the owners of that resource – do not.

The way the web makes money is that it converts our attention into cash. Most commonly that is through advertising, drawing us in with seductive content and then selling the spaces around it to other companies to hawk their wares, who, thanks to the power of modern data analytics, do that

*In a growing economy where our attention
is being farmed for commercial gain,
mindfulness is one of the few tools available
for returning our sense of agency and control.*

in increasingly sophisticated ways. The other principal way attention is turned into money is best demonstrated by so-called 'free-to-play' mobile games. Through engaging gameplay, our attention becomes fixed within a particular experience and the games are designed in such a way that once our attention is trapped we have to pay extra to get a more satisfying or more accelerated experience. Ka-ching!

Mindfulness is also all about attention. In a growing economy where our attention is being farmed for commercial gain, mindfulness is one of the few tools available for returning our sense of agency and control. We should therefore look at meditation as one of the best investments we can make right now. If we continue to invest in mindfulness over time, then not only does our inner capital grow but we also receive some seriously valuable dividends. And unlike the outer attention economy, investment in the inner attention economy is on our own terms.

There was a time when you couldn't learn mindfulness unless you went to Asia. There was a time when you couldn't learn mindfulness unless you were religious or spiritual – and in some places unless you were a man and a monk. But as the years have gone by and mindfulness has changed and evolved, each of these barriers have become redundant, seen through as just being a product of their time. Digital life is today's frontier. *You can't learn mindfulness unless you turn everything off.* Let's see through that one, too.

What you will find in this book

This is a next-generation mindfulness book. At its heart is a fresh, new presentation of mobile mindfulness that meets us where we are and embraces the realities of our modern lives, charger cables and all. By the end you will have all the tools, exercises and ideas you need to go on and bring mindfulness to wherever you are and whatever you're doing. You will also be shown how to go that one step further and design your own meditations. My ultimate ambition for you is that mindfulness might even become natural, a habit so familiar and enjoyable that it takes no effort at all.

This book is packed with practical guidance to help bring mindfulness to life. It is a book you can read in a number of different ways. If you have a specific outcome that you are interested in, such as relieving stress or dealing with difficult emotion, you can jump straight to those chapters. Or you can read the book in order and let the techniques and ideas build upon each other to give you a more complete understanding. You can read the book once and get the inspiration you need or you can keep referring to it as a guide for your meditation practices. Ultimately, it's up to you.

For all the change that mindfulness has enjoyed over the years, the most important moment is here and now with you. Everyone who has ever engaged with meditation has by definition been an innovator. Each of us has a different life and a different set of challenges, so once we learn the basics of mindfulness as presented here, it is up to us to then innovate or apply what we learn to our particular circumstances. After all, at its heart, mindfulness is a creative discipline.

I remember when I first realised that meditation wasn't this distant thing but a set of tools that I could learn and then use to make a difference to exactly where I was. It was incredibly exciting to discover that. I'm just as excited for you and I wish you all the best and more.

How does it feel to hear that? What is happening in the body? What thoughts have just popped into your head? Buckle up. This. Is. Happening.

Chapter 2

This is Relaxation

Do you ever feel like there is just too much information?

A quintillion may sound like a number made up by a three-year-old but it's actually what you get when you put eighteen zeros after a one. Every day over three quintillion bytes are created in our information-laden world. That is a lot of selfies. The incessant generation of data has exploded so much recently that according to IBM research, over 90 per cent of the information that exists on the planet right now was created in just the last two years. No wonder it can sometimes all feel a bit overwhelming.

We all have our own particular challenges, or indeed vices, when it comes to information. For some it is email; for others it is social media or news sites. It is a decent sign of how difficult this all can be that just thinking about the stresses of our modern digital lives can by itself cause even more stress. Alongside any thoughts that might have come up, you might also now be able to notice some tension in the body or some other feelings of discomfort. Oh dear, just reading about stress is stressful, isn't it?

———

One of my meditation heroes tells a story of how the perception of meditation has changed in the thirty or so years in which she's been teaching. Her work requires her to travel internationally fairly regularly and so several times a year she will go back to her native United States. In the early days when the uniformed officials on the immigration desks would ask her what she did for a living, they would look at her rather suspiciously when she said she was a meditation teacher. Begrudgingly they'd let her through with at least one eyebrow raised. But nowadays when she makes the same declaration, the response is entirely different.

You teach meditation? Oh, I could really do with that. I need to be a bit more Zen. Or just as often: *Oh, my husband could really do with that. He's always so busy and needs to learn how to relax.*

Whether it's picking up a book, downloading an app or walking into a class, the number one reason why people get into mindfulness is that they just want to relax. So many aspects of our lives teach us how to be busy, but very few teach us how to unwind. We're overscheduled, overworked, and overwhelmed. Despite all the lifestyle challenges that come about as a result, we are so indoctrinated into the cult of cramming our lives full that we actually wear our busyness with pride. When I see friends and ask them how they are getting on I've lost count of how many times they've responded that they are *busy but good*. I rarely believe them. The tension in their faces tells a different story.

Back in 1965 Gordon Moore, the co-founder of Intel and the then head of research and development, made an observation that is now known as 'Moore's Law'. He stated that advances in hardware technology and engineering are such that the number of components that can be crammed onto a silicon chip would double every eighteen months, and therefore the processing power of computers would double every eighteen months. Since then Moore's Law has become shorthand for the rate of change of modern digital life. Not only is computing power doubling (and more) in speed every eighteen months, it feels like everything else is as well. Open the newspaper and there is another complex global problem to get our heads around. Open the app store and there is yet another social media service or gaming sensation which we just have to get into. Open the inbox and there is a pile of new things to respond to. Open the calendar and there's just no space. And we daren't even check our voicemail. Thanks, Gordon.

The influential technology commentator Clay Shirky says that the main problem we face is not actually information overload but filter failure. He argues that we have always had the challenge of dealing with lots and lots of information but in the past we have designed ways of curating and filtering alongside the growth of the data so that it felt manageable. The problem now is that that co-evolution of information growth and filter-building has collapsed and the lack of investment into dams means that the information is drowning us all. Given that investing in our minds provides us with inner defences in a world with few outer ones, it is no wonder then that more and more people are turning to mindfulness.

The amount of things we have to deal with in modern life and the rise of mindfulness are two sides of the same coin. All the challenges of outside make us feel the need to turn inside. Unless we build up our inner resources to deal with a world out there which feels faster and faster, then here on the inside, at best we'll be stressed out and at worst, we will burn out.

The desire to perfect our outer lives has been one of the main stories of the last fifty years. As a society and an economy we now live in a world that places a lot of value both on the acquisition of material objects as well as on a magazine-cover body. These things are not intrinsically bad things to aspire to, but what happens when we actually get the car, the house, the fame and the abs? For all of its flaws, one of the good things about celebrity culture is that it signals loud and clear that having it all on the outside is not enough. Even if we perfect our outer life, unless we develop our inner life it's only ever going to be a cake half-baked.

Having a strong inner life means that we have built up qualities such as kindness to ourselves, and have reliable access to calm, concentration and joy. We are able to deal with things when times are tough. We typically spend a lot of time and energy working on our outer lives but once we begin investing in the inside we start to realise that having these less visible resources reduces some of the reliance on just getting more stuff to make us happy. Then if we do still end up wanting the car and the partner and status and the phone, we will at least do it with lightness.

So if a trend of the last fifty years has been how we as a society have become fixated on upgrading our outer lives, then a key trend of the next fifty must be doing the same to our inner lives. The alternative is that as our outer technologies continue to explode, our own personal ability to deal with that change will not stay in step. That's where mindfulness comes in. By training in mindfulness we give ourselves a chance of moving towards a Moore's Law for the mind. While we might not be able to double our brain power every eighteen months, if we practise regularly, we will see marked improvements in how we cope with the travails of modern life. And that starts with dealing with stress and learning how to relax.

———

Imagine a life without any stress. Isn't it attractive? We'd float through our days with no worries or concerns. Our family and colleagues would behave in accordance with our wishes. Our relationships would be without friction and whenever we boarded a train we'd get a seat every time. On the outside there would be no negativity in the news to work ourselves up about, and on the inside we wouldn't give ourselves too much of a hard time.

Spoiler alert: it's never going to happen. If life without stress sounds utterly fantastic, then there's the clue right there: it is a fantasy. Stress is just a part of life. It is simply part of the package that starts with birth and ends with the other thing. We have bodies that fail every now and then and at some point give up entirely. We have minds with their thoughts, moods and feelings, granting us experiences that range from the glorious to the truly difficult and everything in between. And if dealing with ourselves wasn't challenging enough, then there are other people. All of this means that stress is just as much a part of life as the rain.

We imagine that we could help reduce stress by simply removing everything stressful from our lives. This is the monastic move. Ditch the job, ditch the relationship and throw our phones into a river. As attractive as this might sound, that doesn't work either. Having spent a fair amount of time in monasteries over the years in various exotic and not-so-exotic locations, I've met several monks and nuns who have told me that stress is not proportional to how many things you have. While they admit that their full-time training has a massive positive impact on their wellbeing, their experience is that just having less stuff does not always make you less stressed. I remember a monk once telling me how he used to be an advertising executive and had the lot, but now only technically owns eight items: his robes, his razor blade, his bowl and a couple of other basic things. But even though he hardly had any material possessions, his stress and worry about material objects then became concentrated in those few items. This all culminated one day early on in his monastic life when he went mental after another monk took his razor by mistake, making him realise that outer renunciation wasn't the same as inner renunciation.

It is also important to realise that stress isn't *all* bad. The emotional and physiological experience of stress is a carefully evolved response, allowing us to be ready to act in moments of heightened alarm and urgency. So when those experiences do arise they are just our minds and bodies doing their job. The stress response and all the symptoms that come with it are considered an inheritance from a time when life-threatening danger merited a suitable amount of heart pumping and blood racing in service of us getting our fight or flight on. The legacy we now carry around no longer conveys a survival advantage. It is now a wellbeing disadvantage.

How we relate to the stress in our lives has a significant bearing on what the actual impact of that stress turns out to be. The most common attitude people have is that stress is harmful and to be avoided and even feared. However, evidence indicates that when we take this view it can become a self-fulfilling prophecy and we are more likely to develop major health problems if we believe that stress will lead to them than if we don't believe that to be the case.

Instead of looking to deny, suppress or escape from stress, by acknowledging it whenever it arises we can start to learn from what it shows us. Only then can it help us transform for the better. This does not mean that we should deliberately cultivate stressful situations for the fun of it, but at least recognise that we have a choice to be positive and that perspective matters.

So if we can't get rid of stress entirely and demonising it gets us into trouble, then what can mindfulness in relation to stress actually do for us? There are two main ways in which mindfulness can help. In a later chapter called *This is Coping*, we shall look at how to work directly with difficult experiences like anxiety, which involves more advanced techniques. So in this chapter we shall learn the other primary tactic which enables us to get by in the face of stress – relaxation.

The first qualities that we begin to develop when starting

out in meditation are the awareness we need to see and acknowledge our stress in the first place, and the sense of calm which gives us the steadiness we need to avoid getting dragged away in the deluge.

Awareness is our ability to directly observe aspects of our physical and mental experience. When our awareness is broad, we are able to observe different aspects of our experience such as sounds, physical sensations, moods and thoughts. When our awareness is deep, we are able to observe things in finer detail. We know there is calm when our mind has an overall sense of quiet without excessive thinking or agitation. Having a good mental baseline of calm improves the signal-to-noise ratio of the mind and makes it easier to notice what is happening. It is also a pleasant experience in its own right.

When we know how to develop these two qualities, they become gifts that keep on giving, helping us to stay relaxed when everything would indicate that there should be stress. And in my own story, it was on a bright Saturday morning, on the eve of the biggest day of my life, that I needed that the most.

———

I crushed myself with my own car the day before my wedding. Not only was it the most idiotic thing I have ever done in my life, it was also one of the best ever tests of my mindfulness practice.

Our wedding weekend was to take place in a beautiful part of the English countryside near where Lucy, my soon-to-be wife, had grown up. Before the main ceremony on the Sunday, we had organised an informal Saturday, full of games, food and meeting old friends and new. There was a lot to do on the morning before everyone arrived and one of my tasks was to go back to my soon-to-be parents-in-laws' house to pick up some things. Having done that, I packed the car and slammed down the boot to close it. Then something happened which I was not expecting. The car started moving slowly forwards down the sloped gravel drive towards the front of the house.

There are lots of things I could have done in that situation. I could have just let the car pick up speed down the drive and hit the front of the house. I could have tried to jump into the car while it was still only creeping forward slowly and pull up the handbrake, which it transpired I had forgotten to set properly in all my busyness. I could have tried to stop the car by pushing it back on the side without putting my body in the way.

But what I actually did was run all the way round to the front of the car to try and stop it full on. It all happened so quickly. And because the car was initially moving so slowly this felt like a reasonable thing to do. Like many people before their wedding I had been a regular gym-goer and I'm sure I was also channelling my inner Hulk. Unfortunately I'm no superhero. Newtonian physics did its work, and in a blink of an eye the car picked up speed and dropped down a little step between the drive and the front of the house. All of which meant that before I knew it I had the best part of a ton and a half of Volkswagen Golf pinning me against the brick wall of the house.

It was strangely quiet. The fact that I didn't seem to be in any strong pain together with the fact that I could wiggle my toes gave me the confidence that at least neither of my legs were broken – to the best of my knowledge at least. It then became clear that I had three main problems. One, there was no one in the house who could come and help me. Two, the house was off a country road so no one could see the situation I was in. And of course three, I was the filling in a Volkswagen Golf and brick wall sandwich and should that continue for much longer, I doubted the pressure on my legs would be very good news.

The first thought I noticed pop up was how much of an idiot I was. The second was that the best thing I could do was shout for help and so I did that in the traditional way. Nothing happened for around ten minutes but then amazingly, after a decent amount of yelling, I was heard through the hedges by an elderly lady who happened to be passing by. She had only a minor freak-out when she came through and saw me, and thankfully fished her hand into my pocket and called the emergency services using my phone.

In those first ten minutes before she arrived, the pressure of the car and the accompanying pain was getting worse and worse. I also noticed how my mind had started spinning out to all kinds of scenarios. Would I be able to walk properly down the aisle the following day? Would I be able to walk at all? Was Lucy OK? How were her parents going to react? Would the cricket pitch be set up in time for the game later that afternoon? I think it is fair to say that I was experiencing a stressful situation.

This is when my mindfulness kicked in. Having done so much practice before, I knew that the thoughts would just spin me out, and so the best thing to do was to drop my attention into my body. What I found there were some really difficult sensations, but I was able to just be aware of the sensations as they were, instead of getting caught in the stories associated with them. So I felt the feeling of pressure in my thighs, not the worry that the car was wrecked. I was aware of the hardness of the brickwork behind me, not the panic that the weekend might be ruined. By deliberately placing my attention in that way, and keeping my mind focused only on the physical feelings in my body, I prevented myself from spinning out into the stories about what was going to happen as a result of the accident, and how I was the worst groom ever.

All the hours that I had spent up to that point doing body awareness techniques bore fruit in that moment. Because I had developed it as a habit and despite the circumstances, I found it relatively easy to drop into just knowing how the body felt, without any judgement and without creating any additional story. That experience really made me understand why when we talk about meditation we call it meditation practice. We call it practice because it gives you all the skills that we require for the times when you need them the most. Despite knowing that I'd done a stupid thing, I also had never felt so grateful for my practice as I did while trapped by my own car. I was breathing with what was happening. Knowing what the breath was like. Letting my mind rest in the body.

Don't get me wrong. It did get difficult. It wasn't until a full forty-five minutes after the initial accident that the car

By training ourselves in less dramatic times, we can build up the skills and habits that allow us to draw upon them at moments of real need.

was eventually hoisted away. In all that time the pressure of the car against my body and the wall was getting more and more intense. When being aware of the sensations became more than I could handle I switched my approach and moved my awareness to where I could notice that which was not painful. I latched my mind onto wherever in the body I could find steadiness or stability, even the tiniest amount. It was a real test but I managed to stay calm. My body relaxed despite all the pressure.

As if that wasn't dramatic enough, I think I also set a new record for the number of emergency vehicles ever to attend an accident in this sleepy Dorset village. The first on the scene was an early response unit from the nearby army base. A police bike, a police car and then a second police car arrived shortly afterwards. Then the fire engine came, followed closely by a second fire engine which left when it saw that its friend had the situation covered. Then the ambulance finally came to give me the medical assessment which was required to hoist back the car. The kicker was that the paramedics said that the serious nature of the accident actually meant that it was necessary to get a doctor's permission to remove the vehicle since it was above the paramedic's pay grade. That is when the helicopter air ambulance landed in a nearby field with the doctor to complete the final sign-off. It was quite a scene. Somehow or other, when the car was eventually removed I managed to hobble away. Nothing was broken and by the afternoon I was in relatively OK shape. The wedding went beautifully, although my dance moves were somewhat inhibited.

This may be a rather extreme example, but it does highlight that not only is meditation valuable in the most stressful of times, but that by training ourselves in less dramatic times, we can build up the skills and habits that allow us to draw upon them at moments of real need.

But we don't have to be trapped by a car to get started; we can do so while doing anything at all. Even while reading a book.

We're now going to switch things up a bit and move into an actual meditation practice which we can do just here as we are. Later in this chapter you will find ten different relaxation meditations which you can try by yourself all throughout the day. But before we get to those let's introduce the first core technique in the book.

So let's get going.

There's no need to move into any special position.

You are great just as you are.

———

Getting out of your head
Core technique #1: Body awareness

Let's start by sensing how relaxed you feel right now.

If you had to rate it on a scale of one to ten, what would it be?

And how do you even know?

Mindfulness is training ourselves in direct knowing. In being aware of what is happening in the moment we are experiencing.

If our attention is on something that is agitated and restless, then we are more likely to become more agitated and restless ourselves. If our attention is on something calm and still, then we are more likely to become calm and still.

How still are you right now?

Can you notice any parts of your experience which are frantic and any which are more quiet?

How are you telling the difference?

I have lost count of the number of long-term meditators that I've met over the years who are really good at being still while doing formal practice but 'off the cushion' are all over the place. Instead of relying on special conditions for our calm, what we are looking to do here is cultivate a more dynamic type of stillness. This means that it doesn't matter if we are moving around or if we are actually physically still, our minds can still be calm and relaxed. The technique that helps us get there is body awareness.

One of the great blessings of life is that despite it being incredibly active, the overall experience of the body is one of relative stillness. Just think of all the high-paced stuff that goes on inside this thing called the body. The blood flow. The firing of neurons in the brain. The cellular processes which create and distribute energy. The constant battle that is our immune system. Imagine if we were aware of all of those things as they happened. It would be just too much.

Thankfully we're only aware of a subset of everything that goes on. We can know temperature such as how cool or warm our face is feeling. We can know pressure such as the feeling of our bottom on the chair or our feet on the ground. We can know tension in our jaw. We can know softness like that which we feel in our face as we smile. We can know pain and pleasure and energy and movement.

So this is the practice. Mindfulness 101 or Basic Knowing. Place your attention on the sensation in your hands as you hold the book.

There's no need at the moment to label the sensation or name it in any way, just feel it and know what that feeling is like.

If this seems outrageously simple and ordinary, then that's because in a way it is. This feeling of holding is happening.

Knowing this feeling is awareness. Know this feeling just as it is. This simple act of knowing is the fundamental unit of the mindfulness universe.

Congratulations. You are now a meditator.

The basic instruction of the body awareness technique is to choose an area of the body and ask what is happening there. Then we let awareness do its work, paying attention to what is happening in our chosen region with as much simplicity as we can.

If we then want to also emphasise relaxation, we notice where there is tension and make the deliberate intention to relax those areas. If we want to emphasise calm, we can prioritise paying attention to sensations or regions of the body which already feel relatively calm or steady.

Let's start with how you're sitting right now.

Simply know how the overall position of your body is as you read this.

The space it takes up. Directly knowing what that feels like.

Just the simple knowing of your physical experience right now in this moment.

There is no need to judge our posture as to whether it is slovenly or sublime, just pay attention to it as it is.

Pay attention in as simple and direct a way as possible right now.

Take as long as you need.

Now we'll move on from the overall sense of the body to the place where you can feel most contact.

If you're sitting down, that will be the contact with your chair. If you're standing up, that will be the contact point of your feet on the ground.

This is most likely a very neutral sensation.

Neither painful nor pleasurable, it is most probably just a bit flat.

Unlike some other sensations, you're unlikely to have much charge associated with it. And as a neutral sensation, there won't be any real desire to push it away and the ordinariness means that we're also not going to want to get all grabby around it. It's nothing special. But it is very grounding.

Being aware of our contact with the chair or the floor literally puts us in contact with the ground. As we become more used to resting our attention here, we develop the ability to ground ourselves on demand at times when we really need it.

Can you still feel it or have you become distracted?

If you've done any kind of mindfulness practice before, it is likely to have involved the breath. The breath, or more accurately the sensations of breathing, is the most common focus of meditation around.

Where can you most notice the breath and its movement right now?

For the majority of us it's most easily contacted in the belly.

Or it can be noticed in the chest and, if you're showing off, you might notice it in the sensations around the nostrils.

Feel free to place a hand on your belly if you're not quite feeling the breath clearly. Having your hand there will give you a much more sensitive contact area to notice.

After posture and breath, the other most classic body awareness technique is called body scanning.

It is just how it sounds. Moving our attention from one end of our body to the other and back again, noticing what we notice. When scanning like this, we will find areas of tension, areas of pleasantness and areas which just feel blank.

You can take as long as you like to do a body scan – anything from thirty seconds to thirty minutes is good.

Let's try one now.

Starting from the feeling of your feet on the ground, move your attention slowly up, taking time to notice what the sensations are like in your feet.

In your calves and shins.

Just asking the question: what is happening?

Know what is happening. Notice any tightness or tingling or heat that is around.

Letting relaxation happen.

Now move up to the thighs and seat.

There may be sensations which don't feel like much. That's OK. Blankness is an experience in itself. It's not that there's nothing there, it's just that there's a feeling of blankness or neutrality there. There is always something happening and all is welcome.

Now move your attention to find out what the upper body feels like right now.

The belly.

The chest.

The neck.

Notice any tension and let it relax.

The lower back.

The upper back.

The shoulders.

Know tension and allow relaxation to happen.

When there is relaxation, enjoy the relief that comes with that.

There's likely to be some more action up here than there was in your lower body. Just notice that there is. Whether it's tension, tingling or nothing much at all.

Now to the head.

Take some time to feel what the jaw and mouth and face feel like.

The jaw and the face are classic places to hold tension.

Notice if there is any tension and relax it when you can. Observing and enjoying the relief.

Do the same for the eyes and the area around the eyes.

Move your attention all around your head, even to places like the ears and nose, and see what can be known there, even if that is blankness.

Then return through the body back down to your feet at your own pace.

There will have been a tendency to rush through the body scan while reading it like this on the page.

All body awareness is a good thing and so that is fine, but there can be real depth gained by taking it slowly, and being super interested in whatever details you can perceive at each station along the way. Taking more time allows us to see more tension, and therefore invite more relaxation as opposed to when we rush on through.

When we do a body scan, quickly or slowly, we are likely to come across some striking sensations. These could be pleasant such as tingling or vibration. But more likely we may find tension or even pain.

Do remember that if paying attention to any particular area is too difficult to handle, then please feel free to move on. Not everything we are aware of in meditation is pleasant and sometimes the wisest thing to do is to move on. In later chapters we shall look at how we deal with difficult experience but our main intention in this section is to develop awareness, calm and relaxation.

So to finish this exercise let's do just that.

Whether it's your posture, the feeling of contact with the ground, your breath or an area somewhere in your body, find something that feels pleasant.

It could be a sensation of warmth, relaxation, tingling, calm, steadiness, anything – even a feeling of neutrality.

Take your time to find something and rest your attention there.

And when your mind runs off into something else just bring it back. This is a hugely valuable skill: training our mind to rest in the lovely.

———

Body awareness is a fundamental technique and there are many reasons why it is the best place to start. While much of our tension manifests in our bodies, many of us spend so much time stuck in our heads that we don't have much awareness of what's going on from the neck down. If we are not aware of our body, then we don't even give ourselves the chance to notice tension when it is present. It often starts quietly and then builds up, only elbowing its way into awareness when it is sufficiently strong so as to be unavoidable. When we have good body awareness we are able to notice tension earlier on in the process and we then have a measure of control. That control allows us to deliberately decide to relax those areas of the body. This all means that we develop the ability to dissipate low-level tension before it gets the chance to gain too much momentum. And because our body and mind are linked in all sorts of ways, if our body remains relaxed then we are less likely to experience stress.

Relaxing the body through meditation can be understood as a three-step process. The first step is knowing that tension is there. Only when we become aware of tension can we move on to the second step and deliberately try to relax it and the area around it. The third step is often ignored but in my opinion it is actually the most important – noticing the relief. When we notice tension and then relax it, even if just

When we are able to keep the mind aware of the simplicity of basic physical sensations, it prevents us getting caught up in thoughts and stories which we might otherwise layer on top of that sensation.

a tiny bit, there is a sensation of relief. When we can notice relief then something really wonderful can happen because the relief of tension is so delicious, like a cool glass of water on a hot summer day. When we see the process of tension-relaxation-relief in full, we start to reinforce a habit which over time means that whenever we notice tension, we start to spontaneously relax in order to enjoy the relief that comes with that. Habits form when we receive some kind of reward from our behaviour. Therefore, making sure we really feel the benefits of our relaxation, and indeed our mindfulness practice in general, we give ourselves the best chance of it becoming habitual and natural.

The second reason why body awareness is such a valuable technique is because it teaches us the fundamental skill of staying at the level of basic sensations. Mindfulness is knowing whatever is happening just as it is. When we are able to keep the mind aware of the simplicity of basic physical sensations, it prevents us getting caught up in thoughts and stories which we might otherwise layer on top of that sensation. For example, if we are feeling tense, one route is to get sucked into the story about what that tension means and how it's always going to be there and how I can't believe he said that and why am I so useless and . . . you get the picture. But when we drop our attention down into the body we can bypass any difficult thoughts that might be there and give ourselves some much needed space.

The third reason why body awareness should be your first mindfulness technique is perhaps the least obvious. What we can be aware of is directly related to what our awareness is like. So if our awareness is subtle, then we can notice aspects of ourselves that are subtle. But if our awareness is relatively coarse, then we won't be able to see all the subtle detail. Therefore, if we were to start out in mindfulness and go straight away to look at thoughts and emotions in detail, then our awareness won't yet be quick enough to keep up. So we start by training our attention on something which moves a little bit more slowly, like the body. Then because we can look at our body in finer and finer detail, we can use it to train our awareness up to the point where it is quick enough and stable enough to look at things like thoughts and impulses.

———

You have now tried out a core technique that can be used either as a formal practice or as the basis for mindfulness in any situation. Here are ten specially designed mobile meditations for you to try, with many of them based on this core practice of body awareness. Because there are so many different opportunities to support relaxation all through even the busiest of days.

Ten Meditations
Designed for relaxing around the clock

 Cyborg Sense

There is an idea from the world of cognitive science called the 'extended mind', which refers to how we outsource bits of our mind to our technologies. Now that we can access so much information through our phones and other devices on demand, we no longer need to keep so much of it in our memory. After all, Albert Einstein did once say that we should never memorise something that we can look up. What if we were to play with that idea, and when doing body awareness practices to think of our phone or tablet as part of our body? The average person checks their phone up to a hundred times a day. That is a hundred opportunities to be aware of our body. The next time you pick up your device, be as aware as you can be about what the physical experience is like. Can you notice the different textures that make up your phone? The smoothness of the touchscreen, the bumps of the buttons, the temperature. Try bringing your attention back to your body in this way whenever you check your phone or tablet. When we bring more awareness to what it is like to hold our phone then every app becomes a mindfulness app.

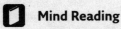 **Mind Reading**

Given that this book is all about learning to practise mindfulness whatever we're doing, this applies just as much to when we're reading. You have now come across the first of the six core techniques but there are other less explicit ways of meditating while reading. Throughout the book you will find these symbols which mark the end of one particular little section and the start of another:

———

The invitation is to use these as reminders to draw your attention back into the body whenever you see them, thereby grounding your attention that little bit more. Not only will it mean you get more out of the content, thanks to your mind being more relaxed, but this idea of using a section break as a meditation reminder can then be used in any book you read from now on. Then just as the body awareness practice when using our devices can turn every app into a mindfulness app, this one has the power to turn every book into a mindfulness book.

 Morning Glory

The first thing we do when we wake up can set the whole tone for our day and should be handled with care. Getting out of the right side of the bed is a choice we can actively make so let's make sure we do. Spoiler alert: the best thing to do with our first moment of waking consciousness isn't check our phone. So here is a little morning routine that is pretty great. When you first remember, ideally when still lying in bed and definitely before you've checked your phone, drop the idea into your mind that you're going to have a positive day just by stating the intention to yourself to do so. Then spend a few minutes scanning your experience for whatever feels the most pleasant – such as a warm or relaxed part of the body or a simple delight in the sounds of nature outside your window. Spend one or two minutes resting your mind on that experience as much as possible. If there's nothing obvious to rest on, just smile – even a fake one works – and notice the simple relaxation and happiness that comes with that. Then when you get up watch how long your warm mood persists and notice what it is that makes it fade away.

Street Feet

Some people find it surprising to hear how back in the day walking meditation was considered just as important as the sitting form. In the most traditional settings it is very common to alternate sitting practice with walking practice, but unfortunately over the years the popular image of what meditation looks like has become reduced only to sitting. Therefore when we start to combine mindfulness with walking we are being both progressive and old school at the same time. And because we spend so much of our time walking from one place to another, it is a perfect activity to use for some invisible meditation. The most straightforward practice is to build our sense of embodiment by putting as much of our attention as we can into the feeling of our feet striking the ground, and bringing the attention back to those sensations when we get distracted. This not only gets us out of our heads for a short time, it can also result in a gentle sense of absorption, especially if done for several minutes. What's more, a lovely thing happens when we do this practice on a regular basis: when we walk we find that our awareness naturally drops into the walking without our having to do anything about it.

 Beditation Time

Just as we can set the tone for our day, how we go to bed can set the tone for our sleep. And if our sleep is particularly restless, that can have a significant effect on how we feel the next day, and on it goes. A way to nudge ourselves into a restful sleep is to keep as much attention in our body as we can, thus dropping out of the busyness of thinking and giving our minds the chance to wind down. Lying down in bed is a signal to our brains that we want to go to sleep. But if we're not giving enough attention to our sprawled-out bodies and are caught up in thought instead, then we aren't giving those signals a fair opportunity. Take at least five minutes to move your attention through your body, from the top of your head to your feet, feeling whatever sensations you come across without creating any stories or making any judgements about them. Feel free to move up and down the body as many times as you like, keeping the movement of the attention fairly slow and allowing it to hang out in areas of the body that feel particularly restful such as in the belly.

School of Breath

This technique takes advantage of the correlation of our breath to our emotions. It's this mechanic that we all intuitively know since we know that one of the best things to do when feeling angry is to take some deep breaths. When you feel the need for more calm, encourage that by intentionally calming the breath by making it longer or deeper. Over time try to notice what your breath is like in different situations and you may find that you can use the breath to help identify moods or emotions before they become fully grown. You can then make your breath longer and more relaxed as a way to encourage your mind to relax. Find out what works for you.

Posture Watch

Just as the quality of our breath can correlate to our mood, so can our posture. When our back is straight we tend to be more alert. When our belly is soft we tend to be more relaxed. When our chest and shoulders are open we tend to be more confident. Check in with your posture on a regular basis, and use that awareness to learn if particular moods match particular postures. That information may well be just what you need to make a posture adjustment which brings a little bit of brightness and energy to your day. Studies have revealed how just by standing in a posture of confidence, even when we don't feel it, can affect testosterone and cortisol levels in the brain. In other words, 'faking it till we make it' does actually work.

61

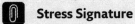

Stress Signature

This is one of the techniques I've used pretty much on a daily basis since I first tried it out about ten years ago. It came about when I first realised that although stress can be experienced all over the body, I tended to feel it in the same places every time. That's what I call my stress signature, the one or two very particular tell-tale places that tighten up each time stress is making itself known. The good thing about this information is that when we know what our signature is we can use it as an early-warning system, deliberately relaxing those hot spots whenever we notice them starting to tighten. If you don't know what they are already, just really pay attention to what it feels like when you're caught in stress. Good places to look would be the most typical signature zones of the face, the jaw, the shoulders, the chest, the belly and the hands. It can also be so useful if we give them some care even if we think we're not feeling stressed. My signature areas are my jaw and my shoulders. So what I do is make sure they are supple and relaxed as often as I remember since it can head off any future tension accumulating.

Whole Body Breathing

All the lists of meditations like this that you'll find in the book will finish off with two formal meditation techniques. It can take some effort to make time for formal practice but when we do, it can really supercharge our overall understanding of mindfulness. To help you along there will be a little tip on ways to get more into sitting meditation at the start of each one, such as this one on posture. Some people say it's OK to lie down when doing formal meditation. I am not one of those people. I don't care if you sit on a chair, a cushion or a massive pile of copies of this book which you very kindly bought, the two key elements are that your back is upright since that encourages alertness and that your belly is relaxed since that encourages openness. While openness is easily accessible when we're lying down, alertness is not. We are too hardwired to associate the lying posture with sleep. So do yourself a favour and try the formal practices when you're sitting down. This particular one is especially good for beginners since it is nice and simple and can actually be quite restful and restorative. It's probably my favourite way to start any sitting meditation and the practice I find especially useful when I'm feeling a bit all over the place.

Start by being aware of your overall posture. How you are sitting. What that feels like. Feeling the stability of the whole body as it sits. Then invite the breath into awareness. Instead of trying to locate the breath in one specific part of the body, know it as an experience that fills the whole body. The whole body as you breathe in. The whole body as you breathe out. Letting the breath feel as full and as relaxed and as natural as possible. Choosing to perceive the whole body as the experience of breathing. Do this as long as you want but I'd recommend at least ten or twelve minutes to give you the most chance to get the full effect. This can be a deeply relaxing and nurturing experience when developed over time. Even a friend for life.

Pleasure Scan

The jury is out as to whether using a meditation timer is helpful or not when doing formal sitting practice. Ultimately it's whether it works for you. Using timers has been useful for me in the past as a way to bring a little bit more discipline to my practice. Then there were other times when using a timer made me feel like meditation was a bit of a chore that I was doing a little mechanically. Quality is always better than quantity and so whether you use a timer or not, make sure that quality is a more important metric than just sitting time. This meditation is a twist on the classic body scan. When slowly moving your attention throughout the body, choose not to concern yourself with unpleasant sensations and instead prioritise the pleasant. This could be an area which is warm, tingly or just nice. Or it could be an area which at first seems blank but is actually just calm or quiet. Just rest your awareness in this area, letting it soak up the whole experience. If you like, you can just stay in one area or move around to find others. This may sound like a self-indulgent exercise, but in the same way as we occasionally have a bubble bath instead of a shower, there are times when what looks like indulgence is just self-care.

Chapter 3
This is Focus

You won't believe how distracted I was while writing this chapter.

Writing a book is hard. Especially when it is your first book and the longest thing you've written to date is an eight-hundred-word blog post. When the mind is faced with anything hard there is a tendency for it to want to move away. It would rather do anything other than stare at a blank screen and so its natural play is to look for a more pleasant experience elsewhere. That is what distraction is. It is the mind saying, *I don't want to be here.* Sitting at my desk and looking closer, I can see that underneath the impulse to escape, the reason my mind doesn't want to be here is a mixture of fear and doubt. The fear of not being able to write and, hot on its heels, the doubt that whatever I do write will be no good anyway. So the mind wants to move away from the unpleasant towards something a bit more enjoyable. That's distraction. And it all happens so quickly.

Despite my best intentions, I notice my fingers twitch away from my keyboard towards the trackpad on their way to opening up a web browser. Some of the arguments as to why I absolutely have to check the latest score in a cricket match being played halfway across the world between two teams I don't even care about suddenly become very compelling. What if an amazing email has popped up in my inbox in the ten minutes since I last checked? Had better have a look then. My hand reaches out for my phone as if moving by its own devices. Before I know it I am scrolling through my Twitter stream at a time when my schedule says I should really be writing. Does this sound familiar at all?

It is too easy to blame all the technology around us for how distracted we are. Throughout history all that the very best technology has done is take something we already did and help us do it better. We were already moving around by horse and cart and the automobile made it easier. We were already keeping food cool in larders and fridges made it more effective. We were already feeling jealous of our successful friends from university and Facebook made it just that little bit more resentment-inducing.

The everyday technology of the internet, messaging systems and our mobile devices is definitely distraction's best friend. But if it was all technology's fault, then if I leave my phone at home and use a clever little bit of software that locks down the internet, I should be perfectly concentrated, right? But I'm not. I convince myself that I need one more cup of tea. Or that I should read yet another article since that would make my book even better. Or that I should go to the super-market before it closes to get my favourite thing for dinner in case they sell out. Despite it never having happened before.

Having looked at my own experience in a fair bit of detail, it is now incredibly clear to me. Every time I become distracted while doing something I have to do, the real reason – the ground zero, the big bang – is a feeling of discomfort. This is important.

When I see this, everything starts to change.

The blank page is now my friend. My body feels relaxed and calm. The universe is made up of my research notebook and my computer. The words start coming and the paragraphs stack up. Every now and then I take tiny breaks where I close my eyes and just relax my awareness back into my body. Focusing my attention on how my body is feeling and being interested in which areas are calling for attention and actively relaxing them. Each break takes no time at all. I know that not everything I'm writing will make it through the edit but there is a gentle productivity and I am getting stuff done. This is what focus is. The mind resting in one place and the simple pleasure that comes about as a result, which then encourages it to continue in that way.

I can still notice the tendency to become distracted. My fingers still twitch towards my phone or my browser. But now I have the stability of mind to just watch that happen and not give into it. Letting the movement of the mind just fizzle itself out thanks to not fuelling it in any way. By the time I finish this section, I've been writing for much longer than I thought.

There are some times when it's OK for my attention to flit from one thing to another but writing is not one of them. It needs my attention to be collected in one place with a certain level of commitment and dedication. When I do take breaks and browse the web, I can see how my attention fragments and becomes jittery as it starts to want to hop from one article to the next. I see how it is so much easier to dissolve my concentration than it is to build it up and so when my mind is fairly collected I do make sure to guard it as much as I can. If I am going to watch a cat video, it had better be worth it.

———

It has been fascinating to watch how mindfulness has become something used by elite sportspeople and athletes to help achieve the level of focus they need to perform at the highest level. This suits our popular idea of what focus or concentration looks like. It looks like Rory McIlroy lining up the putting which wins the major golf tournament. It looks like superstar basketball player Kobe Bryant with his headphones on before a finals game. It looks like Jessica Ennis-Hill heading for the finishing line or Jonny Wilkinson preparing for a kick in a make-or-break rugby match.

Athletes often talk about this thing called 'flow' or being 'in the zone'. The feeling of being completely immersed in an activity, when things come naturally with abundant creativity and a seeming lack of effort. It is a beautiful thing and is something that we mere mortals do occasionally experience. It is most common when we're engaged in something with the right combination of challenge, absorption and joy. We might know it ourselves from activities such as playing music, playing sports, playing on the PlayStation, making art or making love.

But if you're anything like me, life looks less like a Nike

ad and more like a to-do list. My own experience of focus and concentration is all about the need to just get what I need to do finished without going off the rails. I find it useful, therefore, to think about focus not as the elevated experience of flow but as the ordinariness of simply not being distracted. I remember one of my meditation teachers telling me that the prize of practice is best understood not as super-deep concentration but as a non-distracted mind. As with most things, she was absolutely right.

Concentration is one of those things that we can put on a pedestal as being something very special. This can especially become a problem as you develop into a more experienced meditator and start to hear about special states of deep concentration that can become available as your skill increases. I've definitely made the mistake in the past of treating my concentration as something that was overly precious, a special and fragile thing that I built piece by piece, one moment of awareness after another. Despite building it up carefully, like a house of cards I found that one unexpected knock set the whole structure tumbling down. But I've since found that there is a better way. Rather than start from the position that I was naturally distracted and I needed to fix it by developing this special external thing called concentration, I took the more positive perspective that concentration was a natural asset that I already had. When I did that the game changed from being about building concentration up to just keeping a lookout for distractions and letting my attention's natural ability to be steady shine through. This may sound like a small and subtle distinction but in practice it can make all the difference.

I am not gifted at concentration by any measure. I have met people who only have to sit down and close their eyes before they drop into a blissful state of total absorption. That's not my experience but if it is yours, then do feel free to skip ahead. But I'm guessing it's not. There is a very high chance that your mind has been all over the place while reading this chapter. You may even have become distracted whilst reading this paragraph. Or even this sentence. Please don't feel bad about your distraction. You have been well trained in it.

I've already talked about how technology makes distraction easier. There is, however, more to the story than that. Not only does our digital world contain infinite distractions, but it actually *trains* us in distraction. If we are reading a news article or watching a video online, then what we find is that in, over and around it are adverts, photos and clickbait headlines specifically designed to entice us to read or watch anything other than what we actually wanted to read or watch in the first place. What a mess.

When Tim Berners-Lee invented what was to become the worldwide web as we know it today, he designed it as a distributed, highly networked system with no real centre. Thanks to the dominance of the internet and the web, the principles underlying them, such as networking and decentralisation, have become massively influential in all sorts of different aspects of our lives. From how management systems are structured in companies to how taxis get to where you need them, we live in a world where the main model of how we organise things is by putting a little bit of something – be that corporate decision-making power or cars – in lots of places rather than all of it in one place. However, unlike the web or taxis, concentration really only works when our attention is highly centralised, not when it is fragmented. Focus is only possible when we are collected.

I would say that this is mainly advertising's fault. Advertising has won the web. Whether it's access to information, games, messaging or entertainment content, free is now well established as the dominant price point on the web. And given that free is free, the only way to make money on any real scale on the web is via advertising. Our attention has thus become the primary commodity of the digital economy, and the tactics and systems designed to trap it have become an industry worth the best part of one hundred billion pounds. It's time to reclaim ownership of our attention.

This is not a new problem. While our technologies have no doubt accelerated the scatteredness of our attention, there has always been an abundance of distractions. In the fifth century, texts from the Chinese Buddhist tradition talk about the 'monkey mind', a hyperactive awareness that jumps from place to place. And a thousand years before then, Hippocrates of oath fame wrote of patients who had heightened reactions to things, and attention that moved from thing to thing very quickly. He attributed this problem using the language of his time as being due to an overbalance of fire over water but today, when on the more extreme end of the spectrum, it has another name.

Patrick first became aware he had Attention Deficit Hyperactivity Disorder when he was around eight years old, but it was not until much later that it was officially diagnosed. He had been told that he was just a high-energy child but like the majority of children who have symptoms of ADHD it continued into his adult life. Today Patrick is a computer science student and finds it difficult to focus for any length of time when reading or studying. He is also a DJ and he even finds it hard when working on his music despite it being his great passion.

ADHD is a specific diagnosed condition and so much more than the everyday scatteredness that the rest of us know so well in our own lives. But I was particularly pleased when Patrick got in touch with me since when I heard more of his story I realised that his experience of mindfulness would be just as valuable to those of us with a more general level of distraction.

Because I can't concentrate for long periods of time, I find exams even more challenging than they would otherwise normally be. I was being assessed by my university so that I could make sure I received extra time for my exams and that was what got me into mindfulness. The learning specialist assessing my case included meditation as one of the recommendations he gave me for improving my concentration. I'd heard about it as a teenager so I was excited to give it a go.

But because being still for an extended period of time was effectively his challenge, formal meditation was a real struggle since the solution suggested for his problem was not that different from the problem itself. It was during this period while he kept putting formal meditation off that he heard about one of our apps and that it emphasised the mobile approach of overlaying mindfulness onto what you are already doing. His advanced computer science course was just about to start and so he decided to give it a go, recognising that he needed all the help he could get.

Patrick told me that his concentration and overall awareness has now seen a marked improvement, even to the point where he is able to sit through his two-hour computer science lectures with relative ease. He does, however, recognise that he still has a fair way to go and so is keeping it up. His new target is to continue to improve his focus while studying. Patrick has also found other benefits alongside concentration. *My girlfriend used to complain that I wasn't very observant but she's now noticed a change.* His practice has helped him, in his own words, become *more thoughtful and caring.* When I asked him whether it had affected his DJ-ing in any way he said that because he felt he was now more open to and appreciative of other types of music that had helped him with his overall creative flow.

Given that Patrick is a computer science student I was also keen to get his take on whether there was a relationship between technology and ADHD. While there is no evidence that shows certain technology use causes ADHD, Patrick definitely agreed that it does not help. *It's things such as phone notifications and having multiple browser tabs open that I find most distracting.* He also agreed with me that the solution is not to turn everything off but to actively work with it to support our attention rather than deplete it. Patrick's experience of mindfulness so far has given him the results and the confidence he needed to carry on his own campaign against distraction.

When meditation is done well it trains us in non-distraction, and helps us to recognise the value of non-distraction. Cultivating our mind's ability to rest where we want it to can have immensely positive results. When we're not distracted we are able to listen to others deeply, and are less likely to miss the thing that they are really trying to say. When we're not distracted we are able to perform our work and other tasks in a timely and efficient manner. When we're not distracted we create the conditions for creativity and flow. Training in non-distraction is the investment opportunity that you don't really want to miss. If online advertising is worth a hundred billion pounds, what is the price of our attention?

Non-distraction, in addition to its other benefits, is central to being able to develop further in our overall meditation practice. If having a good sense of awareness allows us to shine a light on our experience, then non-distraction means we can hold that light in one area and see the detail. Our stability of mind can help us understand how our mind works in the first place.

When we do look at that detail we become more interested in how concentration works and we begin to appreciate that there is more than one type of concentration. First up is the one most people think of when it comes to focus, what I have given the somewhat technical name of 'single-object concentration'. This is what we have when we can keep our attention on a specific object for a sustained period of time, such as the physical sensations of breathing. This is the type of concentration most useful for task-based work like writing a report or painting a bedroom wall or performing eye surgery.

The second type of concentration is perhaps a little less obvious and what I call 'field concentration'. There is still an object – a thing that we're paying attention to – but it is not one specific item or activity but a whole field of sensory experience such as all sound or all physical sensations. This can be a much more open and relaxed experience when compared with single-object concentration, and allows us to be aware of more facets of the experience. Field concentration is an inclusive type of concentration compared to the single-object mode, which by definition excludes all experience other than the single object of focus. A good way to differentiate the two is the metaphor of clouds and the sky. Single-object concentration means we focus on one particular cloud and field-object concentration has us resting our awareness with the overall container of the sky (which of course still includes the clouds but is much bigger). More practically, field concentration is the style of concentration we are more likely to use while driving, when we need a panoramic awareness (cars behind us, pedestrians, the road ahead, directions, weather conditions) and not to focus on just one thing.

It can take work to build up our capacity to focus in either of these two ways. When we already love the thing we're focusing on then that positive feeling makes it easy for us to keep our attention on the task. However, most of the time we tend to find our appointed task boring or ordinary or difficult or unpleasant. That is exactly the gap that distraction needs to sneak in. This then is the secret of focus: we must do whatever we can to get over that hump of it being boring and instead somehow make it enjoyable. Interest is the fuel for concentration and by understanding distractions they start to lose their power.

It is also important to remember that focus isn't only a thing we need at work. Being present, connecting with others and possessing the ability to cope with difficulty are all important. The practice you're about to do, therefore, is as useful at home as it is for the office.

―――

Coming back to the object again and again
Core technique #2: Breath-based concentration

How focused do you feel right now?

How often have you lost your place or the meaning of the words while reading the last few pages? How often have you spun out into thinking about something else entirely?

Training ourselves in concentration is a dance. First there is the work of becoming more used to resting the mind in one place. Then we also learn about how distraction works. Through both skills we become adept in staying steady in the place we want to be. Then distractions are no longer the enemy of concentration but its training ground.

There will be points during this meditation where you might get distracted. There might even be something that requires your urgent attention and presence. That's OK. If that happens, just come back to where you left off.

So now, taking as long as you want, go ahead and take three deep breaths.

One.

Two.

Three.

Just this simple act encourages a little bit of steadiness that we can use as the foundation for our concentration practice.

Do it again. Just hold this book and breathe. Three deep breaths. Three long breaths.

Feel the simplicity of that, and enjoy that simplicity.

There are three reasons why the breath is so good as an object for training our awareness. The first reason is the most simple: the breath is always present. As long as we're conscious and alive, our body and our breath are always here and available.

The second reason is that breath can be a mirror to our mood. You already know how the breath can correlate to our mindset. If we're tense, our breath will be short. If we're deeply relaxed, then our breath is likely to be long and relaxed. This ability of the breath to act as an indicator of our mental state means that if we intentionally take deep breaths, we can give ourselves a chance to calm down.

The third reason why the breath is so useful as a meditation object is that it has layers of subtlety. As we become more experienced in meditation we can start to notice a lot of detail within the breath, which means that it can be as useful an object for our attention on day ten thousand of our meditation career as it is on day one.

Your breath can be your best friend in the adventure that is mindfulness. It also helps your meditation be entirely invisible if you want it to be. If you do want to do a version of this meditation when at work, then there is no need to sit astride your desk with legs crossed, signalling to the world, *Hey, look at me, I'm meditating over here*. It's OK now and then to use meditation as part of a work break and there's an extra deliciousness that comes with knowing that we're meditating with no one ever realising. I do it all the time.

What was the one place in your body where you felt the breath the most when you were taking those deep ones? If you're not sure, then just do it again.

Chances are that it will have been either in the movements of the belly, the movements of the chest or, if you were being particularly eagle-eyed, in the sensation of the air as it came in around the nostrils and upper lip.

No place is any better than another. Just take a moment to clock where you know the sensations of the breath most strongly right now. If it helps, you can close your eyes for the next three breaths. Or if you're struggling right now to connect with your breath, you can put a hand on your belly to make that connection more obvious.

This will be your single object. Keep your eyes open and just put as much of your attention as you can into the sensations of breathing where you can feel them the most.

See if you can rest your attention there rather than hold it there against your will.

When doing that for a short time, after just a few seconds you will no doubt be dragged away. Dragged away by another sensation, a thought, a fantasy or some doubt that you aren't doing it very well or in the right way. This is a distraction. Get used to them. And every time you notice that your awareness is no longer on the simplicity of the breath, just bring it back.

This is the start of concentration training. It is the simple and persistent work of placing our attention with the breath, noticing when it's skedaddled away and then bringing it back each time without judgement or a sense of uselessness. So much of modern life is designed to distract us that it is no wonder we're very skilled in being distracted. This is the start of resistance. The start of the fight back. It may take time to feel like you're making progress so be gentle on yourself if your first step towards concentration is finding out that you have none.

Let's try again. Place the mind on the breath. Wherever you feel it most.

Rest with the breath. Setting the intention that your focus will stay in one place.

Noticing distraction. Being alert to that moment when the mind darts away.

Bringing it back. Resetting that intention.

And repeat.

There's no need to criticise yourself if you feel you're doing badly. Nor indeed do you need to organise a ticker-tape parade for yourself if you think you're doing well. Just rest with the breath to the exclusion of everything else. Making it the most important thing in the known universe.

If it helps and you feel OK about it, you can close your eyes. But it's also perfectly doable while your eyes are open, and you're holding this book. If I can do it while

I'm writing, then you can definitely do it while you're reading.

Ignore the details of any distractions for now and use them solely as reminders to start again. Resting the mind on the breath for as long as you can. Sometimes that is quite a while; sometimes it's no time at all. Either is fine. That is just how things are right now.

Let's see if you can keep your focus for the duration of this short paragraph. Locating the breath and resting the awareness there. Feeling the breath come in and then make its way out. The gentle rhythm of that. Just a few more words to go. Lovely stuff.

Some people approach concentration with a lot of machismo. *I will become concentrated, I will, I will.* It is possible to muscle our way to focus, bringing the mind back again and again until the habit really lands. There can be a lot of value to that, and at the start of our adventures in concentration it can feel like we are really forcing things. The downside of training with that kind of machismo is that we can become really tight. We can have all our awareness locked onto our breath for minutes and even hours at a time, but all the while our fists are balled up, our jaw is clenched and we're wracked with tension from the very effort of it all.

If we are looking to deepen our concentration in a softer and more generous way, we can do that by looking again for the lovely. It can be much easier to become absorbed in something if we find it pleasurable. This is a secret to building our focus: we look for the most pleasant or pleasurable aspects of the object of our meditation and use it as our way into deepening our non-distraction.

Go back to the breath while reading this. There may not be any waves of bliss spontaneously arising in your awareness – at least not yet. But if you look closely, and with the stability you might have from these first few paragraphs of practice, there are some aspects of the breath that can be recognised as positive.

Can you notice the calm that accompanies the gentle rhythm of the movements of the breath? Or the natural relaxation of the out-breath?

Maybe there is a sense of stability from having committed yourself for these last several minutes. Or even something like a sense of warmth?

See if you can tune into any positive qualities, however quiet, as if you were tuning an old-fashioned analogue radio. When you find anything that feels positive, even if that is very faint, just seeing if you can emphasise that aspect while staying connected to the breath.

This may be a bit of a trick but it's a very good trick. Develop a little bit of concentration using the breath, and then look for anything about the breath that is lovely, and use that loveliness as a way into deeper concentration.

Now that we've become used to concentrating on just one thing – the breath in a particular place – let's switch it up by trying out the other type of concentration. Field concentration.

We do this by staying with the breath but this time inviting the whole of the body to be our object of focus. Not just a single part of the body, but the whole field of physical sensations as felt by the entire body. This is called 'whole body breathing'.

While earlier we were in touch with the belly or the chest as it expanded and contracted with the breath. Now we do the same but with the whole body. Since the breath helps oxygenate every cell in the body it can be helpful to imagine that the whole body is involved in breathing, like one big balloon softly inflating and deflating.

As you sit here reading this, see if you can feel the breath move out from your core to the tips of your fingers. Letting the full experience of the body be your object. Looking for the lovely, and letting the loveliness, the calm and the pleasure deepen your concentration even more.

———

While not many of us suffer from ADHD, we are all at the very least well trained in distraction. Therefore developing our capacity to focus can feel like an uphill struggle at first. That is entirely natural and so you needn't worry. It can take time to rewire and reinforce certain neural patterns. So there

Remember that fun is one of our secret weapons in turning mindfulness into a habit.

may be times when we have to work hard and we should also be ready for our fair share of failure on the way to success. That's as true for mindfulness as it is for any other skill worth developing or game worth playing.

We've seen how brute force alone works OK when it comes to concentration but the magic happens when we're a bit cleverer than that. There are two secrets to accelerating your way to a less distracted mind. The first is to catch the movement of distraction before it is too far down the chain. This means that we should pay extra special attention to what the feeling is like before we get distracted. Most of the time, what causes us to be distracted is some kind of uncomfortable feeling and moving our attention away to something more fun is in some way actually a compassionate act to ourselves. If we can notice what it is that triggers our distraction while it is happening, then that will give us a better chance of catching ourselves earlier in the process. Sometimes this is a feeling of boredom or dullness but it can also be something more acute like strong emotion. When we grow our mindfulness skills to the point that we can not only identify an initial unpleasant feeling but also just let it come and go, then non-distraction becomes a default way of being.

The second secret to concentration training is enjoyment,

pleasure and fun. If resting the mind in one place feels like really hard work, then of course we find it difficult to come back repeatedly – there's no incentive! It can become much easier if instead we take something we find pleasant or calm as the object of our attention. This can be done either by looking for a pleasant aspect of something like the breath or a body sensation or deliberately choosing something we find naturally enjoyable, such as a feeling of warmth. Remember that fun is one of our secret weapons in turning mindfulness into a habit.

Ten Meditations
Designed to help you spend your days with less distraction

 Advert Jiu Jitsu

Jiu jitsu is the Japanese martial art which is based around the idea of defeating opponents by using their own energy against them. For the context of this exercise, our opponent is advertising. The idea is quite simple: to use adverts as a reminder to go back to what we're doing. So whether we're on the train, watching television or browsing the web, whenever we notice an advert, think of it not as a cue to get caught up in the product message, but as a cue to come back to the present moment. This can take some practice – especially when online – but there is something delightfully subversive about taking that which has been designed especially to distract us, and using it to support our focus and our presence. As we become more skilled in this idea we can use even more types of advertising as reminders, such as shop names and brand names on clothes.

Mouse Sweeper

As I mentioned, mobile mindfulness allows us to be stealth meditators. By working on all of these techniques, no one knows that we're actually meditating while eating, walking or, in this case, working. This technique is a bit of a game which you can use when you want a little break at work. Its genius is that it actually looks as if you are still working, when in fact you are playing a little concentration game. When working at a laptop or desktop computer, move the cursor around using your mouse or trackpad. Keeping your eyes, jaw and face relaxed, keep your attention on it as it moves, letting your ability to track the cursor be the most important thing in the world. Then while you're doing that move your awareness out from the local detail of the cursor to the global container of the screen. When keeping the screen in awareness, try not to look at anything in particular, resting instead with the sense of the screen as a whole. Switch back and forth between the single-object focus on the cursor and the field-object focus of the screen. You can make it more interesting/ harder by doing this on a screen where you normally find distractions such as a news homepage or your Facebook news feed. Remember that meditation is about learning and try and see what you can learn about what distracts you and what doesn't.

📎 Meeting Hands

I don't know if you've noticed yet but meetings at work are really boring. Everyone I've ever met cannot stand meetings but yet we still spend hours and hours in them every month or even week. I stumbled upon this technique during a particularly dull meeting when I realised that it would be very rude to yawn and that I actually did need to pay attention. Clasp your hands together and place your attention on the feelings in your fingers and hands. Keep your mind there as much as you can. Doing this seals up those gaps in our mind where our attention tends to leak. The workplace is rife with opportunities for creating fun little meditations like this one because we spend so much time there and, let's be honest, where else is there so much boredom, stress and frustration ready to be transformed?

📎 Speak Distraction

Noticing *when* we become distracted is as important as encouraging our minds to rest in one place. This meditation uses the practice of 'noting', which we will explore further in a later chapter. Don't let its outrageous

simplicity or unusual mechanic put you off, it is very
effective indeed. The basic idea is that whenever we
notice that we've become distracted, we say the word
'Distracted' out loud. Yes, really. If you work in an open
-plan office or an otherwise busy environment, you can
say the word internally to yourself, but it is most effective
when said out loud. This simple action can teach us
not only about how often distractions arise, but also if
there are any particular patterns to watch out for in the
future. Examples of these patterns might be how we find
ourselves more prone to distraction when we are tired or
frustrated.

 ### Link Blinks

When it comes to ordinary body processes used as meditation objects, breathing tends to get all the attention,
while the humble blink gets none at all. Personally, I have
had an obsession with blinking for a number of years
now. Blinking has a lot of the ingredients that you need
in a good meditation object: it's ordinary, it's always
around and it's nearly entirely invisible. This exercise is
perfect for use at times when you are by yourself, doing
either something active such as desk-based work or something more passive such as commuting. The idea is simply
to see how many consecutive blinks you can be aware of
at any one time, counting them if that feels OK to do.
Don't try to change how you blink; just let it happen however it happens, and notice what it's like. It is a slightly
different experience doing this while engaged in some

other activity to doing it in a more dedicated way, so do play around with it. It's strangely addictive and you might also find that paying attention to the area around your eyes can teach you a lot about how tired you're feeling.

 Natural Lullaby

While focus and concentration are most often associated with the more active parts of our day, the same techniques can be just as useful when we're trying to do the most passive thing we do: fall asleep. One of the main reasons that so many people have difficulty sleeping is that their minds are still very active at the point of wanting to go to bed. We can use concentration practices to settle the mind down and encourage sleep. An effective way to do this is to use the breath to rock ourselves to sleep. A regular rocking rhythm is something we've associated since babyhood as conducive to switching off. The wonderful thing is that we can use what we've learnt about breath meditation to mimic this rocking. We do it by placing our hand on our belly in the same way we'd put our hand on a cradle and just rest our awareness with the sensations we feel there. This is a deliciously simple practice, and by remembering to bring the mind back whenever it drifts away, it just works.

 Park Bench

This is one of my absolute favourite techniques, and it is best done when sitting on a park bench or at any other time when you've got the wonderful combination of having both some time on your hands and a decent view. After establishing some awareness in your posture, with your eyes open and your back alert and relaxed, rest your awareness with the overall visual field just to settle down. Making sure the eyes and face are relaxed, try not to look at anything in particular but to pay attention instead to the overall vista. This is another example of field-object concentration, this time with the visual field. There will be times when something catches your attention such as the movement of a bird or a thought about what you're doing later that afternoon. Whenever you notice that happening just lean back into the bench and reset your mind with the wider sense of all that can be seen. This style of meditation was developed by some pretty hardcore meditators up in the Himalayas, but it's just as useful during a lunch break at work.

Step Tracker

This is another practice based on the best of old-school walking meditation. Walking has always been one of my favourite activities to turn into a meditation practice since it can give us the mental space from everyday thinking that we need to be creative. Try using a simple two-word phrase such as 'be well' or the more mundane 'left, right' or 'one, two' and say the words quietly to yourself in time with your steps. Coordinating our steps with words like this acts as a 'moving mantra', and if done consistently over a few minutes or even longer, it can lead to a dynamic and vibrant style of concentration.

People who use smart watches or other devices to track their steps commonly have a target of ten thousand steps a day. If we could be aware of even a fraction of those steps at the same time, we'd level up our mindfulness skills in double quick time.

Breathing Counts

Whenever I'm asked when the best time to do formal practice is, I always answer this: whenever you can actually do it. Not all of us have the luxury of lots of free time in the day so take what you can get. Generally, however, I've found that there are four main times of the day that work best for people. The first is in the morning before the day has begun. This is particularly good since the mind is generally at its freshest, although that depends on what you might have done the night before. Sitting practice also makes a good break during the day but only really works if you have access to a space where you won't be disturbed and where you're comfortable. Then there's that gap between the work day and the rest of your evening. This is definitely a good time, but many of us have dependants which means that there isn't the time or space for meditation. The fourth and final slot is last thing at night. This late evening slot and the early morning slot are the two most popular, but at night the downside is that the mind can be tired. Whenever you do it, this technique is all about counting the breath, which has been a classic concentration exercise for many years because it just works. The simplest version of counting is to mentally note 'one' on an in-breath and 'two' on the out-breath, repeating it for as long as feels OK. This is relatively straightforward, and the exercises can be made more difficult by counting 'one' on the in-breath and 'two' on the out-breath, and then progressing all the way up to ten. It is, however, most likely that you will become distracted before you get remotely close to ten – in which case just start again. Make sure you are being honest with yourself if you get distracted. Try doing this for ten minutes and see how high you can count. Once you become more skilled in concentration you can increase the complexity even further by counting up to ten, then back to one, then up to nine, and back to one, and so on until you get back to one. When you get to the stage where you can do this without getting distracted then you're in great shape.

 Listen In

Formal practice is sitting down in relative silence and taking a long hard look at yourself. It can therefore be quite hard work. So just as we use stabilisers when learning to ride a bicycle, sometimes we need a little bit of support to get used to the general feeling of meditation before doing the full version. That's the point of this practice and it's one I use fairly often when I feel like I don't have quite enough stability for a classic silent practice. I came up with it after thinking about how common it is now for people to use guided audio meditation exercises as a way to support their formal practice.

This technique takes that idea, and gives it a little twist. Download a favourite podcast – ideally one that lasts about fifteen to twenty minutes. Now sit in a stable meditation posture, either on a chair or on the floor, and start listening to the podcast. Headphones are ideal since the more intimate quality of the sound allows for fewer distractions than a speaker. Just listen to the content as closely as you can for the duration of the podcast. Taking the podcast as the meditation object in this way requires us to stay with the audio and its meaning. You will notice that your mind gets distracted from the content and when that happens just bring it back. If you miss some of the content entirely, rewind to where you got lost. Then just close the session when the podcast finishes. Not only is this a good way of training in concentration, it also trains us to sit in the formal meditation posture for twenty or so minutes at a time, which is very useful. Podcasts work much better than music since they require our mind to stay agile by following the meaning, and it's clearer to us when we become distracted. When we're ready we can increase the length of time we listen for up to thirty or forty-five minutes. This is a great way in, if you find the idea of classic silent formal practice daunting. Another good way to prepare yourself for a tra-ditional formal practice is to set it up so you have fifteen minutes' worth of podcasts and then rest in the silence afterwards for as long as you are comfortable.

Chapter 4
This is Being Present

We're all so obsessed with the now. Just a shame it's the wrong now.

Twenty-four-hour news cycles. Real-time messaging. Social media streams in the palms of our hands endlessly spewing the latest thing we have to know about. This is the stuff of the wrong now. The wrong now is the one that makes us wish we were somewhere else. Makes us feel that there is always just one more thing that we need before we'll be truly happy. One more conversation that we have to be involved with. One more snippet of gossip from our friends that we have to know. The wrong now is the now of elsewhere.

Giving into the wrong now creates a fear of missing out. When we place more importance on what we could be doing rather than what we actually are doing, then what comes up is restlessness and dissatisfaction. By buying into the idea that life would be so much better if we were just doing something else, we place ourselves on a hamster wheel that spends all of our energy and never actually gets us anywhere.

Wanting to be in another now is a game we can never win. It is always possible to imagine an experience that is better than this one here. Wouldn't you be having so much more fun if you were playing the next level of your favourite game or checking into Facebook to see yet more puppy photos rather than reading this book? What if there's a massive news story that has just broken that you don't know about yet? What if you've got some messages waiting in your online dating inbox from the person who ends up being the love of your life? Can you feel it? Can you feel the pull? That's what the wrong now feels like.

The right now is this one. It is what is happening in your experience as you read this sentence. It is how your back feels right now. It is the tiredness you can feel around your eyes. It is the thoughts that are coming up as you read. It is what some people call the present moment. It is a magical thing.

Think about a time in the last few months when you have felt most alive. Most likely that will have been when playing with a child, out in nature, listening to music, having sex, watching a sunset, playing sport or at a concert or event. What connects all these types of activity is that when we're in them, their immediacy and energy mean that at no point do we want to be elsewhere. There is no wrong now, only the right now. Only direct unmediated experience. The simple knowing of what is happening.

Hanging out in the right now is what we mean by being present. And it is a real skill. Not all parts of our lives are as overwhelmingly engrossing as when our favourite band is playing our favourite song on the main stage at the Glastonbury Festival. It is no wonder that we get seduced into another now. And just being somewhere physically is certainly no guarantee of presence. We have all been in situations where our bodies happen to be there but our minds are anywhere but. Therefore presence is the coming together of the two. Body. Mind. Here. Now.

I used to wonder why this present moment thing was such a big deal. But getting into meditation helped me realise that it was the key to everything. It is no accident that this chapter is at the heart of the book. When there is presence we are less likely to become distracted. When there is presence we become more literate in our feelings and patterns. When there is presence the ordinary has the chance to become beautiful. Life puts on the best parties. Being present allows us to actually turn up.

Perhaps what I've found most valuable from developing my own sense of presence is the self-awareness that accompanies it. When we're not present then we have no chance of knowing what's going on inside. Personally, I'd rather be aware of what is going on inside me than not, even though not everything I see will be pretty. Being present means I have a better relationship with my body and am able to listen when it needs attention. I also have a better relationship with my mind, which becomes more sensitive to the play of thoughts, moods and patterns – I am finally more able to see them for what they are. And it almost goes without saying, but I have a better relationship with others since I'm really with them when I'm with them.

There is an old-fashioned idea that the less we know, the better life is. Mindfulness shows us that this is not the case. Ignorance is not bliss. Ignorance is ignorance. When it comes to our inner lives, the less aware we are, the more likely we are to be led by our habits rather than a more conscious choice. This isn't always easy. It is true that sometimes we can become aware of difficult thoughts, such as certain types of negative thinking and impulses that we wouldn't necessarily want to tell our grandmothers about. But since they are in there anyway, it is only through seeing them that we can start to acknowledge, own and work with them. Otherwise these impulses are going to just keep pushing us around and will remain outside of our control. Presence opens the door to mastering these habits.

There was a time when if you asked me how I was doing I would always just say that I was doing OK. *Fine, thanks.* While that wasn't necessarily untrue, it did mask the fact that I was pretty much emotionally illiterate. Having never really bothered to take the time to get to know my inner life in any detail, all I used to see was blankness. At the time I took this to mean that I didn't have much of an emotional life and that was just one of those things. But what was really happening was that I just wasn't looking closely enough. In fact, I wasn't looking at all. By growing my self-awareness through meditation I began to see that there was a whole universe of experience happening within me which I continue to explore today. And that is only possible through presence.

Neuroscience tells us that the ordinary default mode of our brain's network is wandering off: the engine idling away with planning and remembering and daydreaming. There is, however, a more active mode, a so-called 'task positive mode', which is made up of entirely different parts of the brain. These are the parts activated when we are more directly engaged. Planning, remembering and daydreaming are all valuable things to do, but research shows that people are generally happier when they spend more time with their brains in task positive mode. So cutting through the neurobabble, meditation helps us be more present and, even though it sometimes means we become aware of difficult aspects of ourselves, being more present generally makes us happier.

—

Amy had been an administrative assistant in a large law firm for three years when she first got in touch with me. Even though she turned up for work every day, she was never really there. While she got along well with most of her colleagues, she remained disconnected from her job and would spend her time thinking about anything but what was actually happening.

What class is on at the gym tonight? Can I be bothered to go? What shall I get my nephew for his birthday? When will I next get the chance to go over and see them? I should really go and fix the broken screen on my tablet this lunchtime. Where shall I go on holiday next? It was a well-trained pattern. *I'd rather be anywhere but here.*

There were parts of her job that she really enjoyed but most of the time Amy was just going through the motions. She had always wanted to make a difference and had once dreamed of being a paramedic but it never came to anything. After university she needed a job to help pay off her student debts and this was the first one that she had gone for. She had been there ever since. *This is just what work is like, isn't it? Do what you need to do to get the pay cheque and life starts when you leave the office.*

Amy told me that she had been introduced to mindfulness through a friend. One of her close friends had recently done a mindfulness course to help with his anxiety and was telling Amy all about it. *He wouldn't stop going on about it so I finally agreed to download an app he'd recommended and go along with him to a group. I'd heard about mindfulness and was interested but I didn't really do anything about it until he made me. I'm glad that he did.*

The change wasn't immediate; it came gradually. *It was quite an eye-opener.* Amy always knew that she only tolerated her time in the office but what she didn't realise was that it was also making it easier for her to be absent in other parts of her life. She had understood the key insight of mindfulness: we are *always* training ourselves, mostly without even being aware of it. Amy didn't like what she was training herself in, and so decided to do something about it. She made the simple decision to become more present at work and then see what would happen. When she did, she noticed three things.

What Amy noticed first was how not present she actually was. She always knew she was a daydreamer but Amy didn't realise how scattered her mind was until she started meditating. It really shocked her.

The second thing Amy noticed was that when she

deliberately became more present her job wasn't actually that bad. Some of it was still pretty dull, but there were many more moments of real enjoyment and humanity than she had previously realised. It wasn't necessarily her dream job but she made the intention to make the most out of it while she actively started to look for other options.

The third thing she noticed was how the way she behaved at work influenced the rest of her life. By becoming more present in the office, she realised that she had become a better listener. Amy's sister lives on the other side of the world and although she cherished the times they would speak on the phone, Amy noticed how often she would zone out on the call. But over time, as her presence and connection to what was actually happening grew, she saw that her time speaking with her sister became more and more meaningful.

When Amy wrote to me, I recognised much of my own experience in her story. Over the years we become so well trained in not being present that it can feel like an uphill struggle when we first begin practising mindfulness. You would think that it would be easy to give your attention fully to what is happening when you are spending time with a close friend or partner. But what I noticed was that in the first year or so of my relationship with my wife, my own attention would often drift away when we were together, even to the extent where I would reach for my phone. This didn't go down well.

Presence with another person then became a skill I deliberately started to cultivate. This involved me asking myself: how can I be more present with this person right now?

Working with this question has made a big difference, and while my wife wouldn't now say that I am a perfect husband, she would say that I'm a better one. As we'll explore in more detail later, mindfulness is very much a social activity. It can be very helpful to have friends who are also into mindfulness whose support and encouragement can help keep our practice keen. But just as valuable are trusted people who might not be into mindfulness themselves but who we can ask for feedback on our levels of presence. *When we spend time together, do you feel like I'm there or do I ever come across as distracted or distant?* This is a great question to ask someone you trust and are comfortable with, since we have to be OK if the answer isn't what we want to hear.

Keeping in touch with what is happening can take energy on our part. Since our default mode is not to be present, we need to put in effort so that the other more active mode grows in strength and has a chance to become our new default state. So I'm going to share with you my personal favourite core technique in the whole book. This technique – again to be done while reading – has really helped me rewire some of my most persistent habits.

Knowing processes as they happen
Core technique #3: Six-sense noting

You've already done a little bit of body awareness, so let's start there.

Take a few seconds to rest your attention on whatever aspect of your body feels most prominent.

It might be the breath.

It might be the sensation of holding this book.

It might be the overall sense of how your body posture is right now.

Whatever it is, let's start this meditation by grounding our attention in the body.

Body awareness is a classic home base from which to start any meditation. Knowing the simple sensations just as they are right now.

Notice any areas of tension that you might find across your body.

And instead of pushing those sensations away, bring a little bit of interest and acceptance to them.

Now place your attention with the body as a whole.

This is touch.

Touch and physical sensations as a whole are one of the six ways in which we receive information, one of the six channels of experience. In this meditation we're going to explore all the six channels and once we've done that, we will use a supporting technique called noting which was first mentioned in the previous chapter.

That's all to come. But right now, let there just be the knowing of what it is to have a body, just as it is right now.

The next channel we're going to turn our awareness towards is hearing.

The ability to pay attention to sound is a meditator's best friend because hearing requires our minds to be naturally open. So let's do that now.

Sitting or standing comfortably, just as you are, switch your awareness over to the hearing channel.

What sounds can you notice?

Are you able to let sounds come and go? Or do any particular sounds make you jump onto them, naming them or creating little stories around them? If that happens, it's totally fine. The key is not what happens but that you're able to notice what happens.

With your eyes open or closed, try spending a minute or so right now just listening to sounds.

In that time, you may have noticed how your mind wandered away. You may have noticed a tendency to go out to the sound rather than letting it come to you. You may have noticed thoughts flock around a sound, trying to give it meaning or a story.

Let's do it again, taking a minute to just listen with your mind open wide, receiving sounds like a satellite dish.

This is hearing.

The third channel of experience that we have available to us is seeing.

Keeping your eyes and the area around your eyes relaxed, look at the word on the following line.

Family.

A word is a strange thing. At its most basic level a word is just a set of marks on a page. If we speak the language in which the word is written, then it also has meaning. Reading the word 'family' will very likely have brought up some thoughts and images related to your own. All this makes it hard to see it just as marks on a page.

Now let's do the same thing with a different word. Keeping the eyes relaxed, look at the word on the following line just as it is.

Yaflim.

Notice if there was any difference between seeing a word which has a lot of meaning as opposed to one which has little. Notice if your mind tried to spin a story about what the word meant. Isn't it interesting how that happens?

Once you finish this sentence, raise your eyes away from the page and just look at the space around you for a short while.

Some things you see might suck in your attention so notice if that happens. If it does, just bring your awareness back out into the whole visual field. Not making anything more important than anything else.

In some traditions there is a long history of meditating with your eyes open, but in popular culture meditation is often presented as something we do with our eyes closed. Given our emphasis on mobile mindfulness, that is not only a rather unsafe thing to do, it also means we are closing off a whole channel of experience.

Let's not do that. With the eyes open and the face relaxed, let your attention rest mainly in the visual field. However it is right now.

Rest with the full field of visual experience. Don't let anything be more important than anything else.

This is seeing.

The fourth and fifth channels of experience are smelling and tasting. These channels tend to get activated at specific moments of the day such as during meals and when walking through Duty Free at an airport. Most of the time, though, it can seem as if these channels are not active at all. But, of course, blankness or neutrality is still an experience, just a not very noisy one.

So let's see what's happening by switching to the smell channel, being aware of what we can notice through our noses, even if that's not much at all.

This is smelling.

And the same for tasting. Tasting is so close to smelling and indeed to feeling. Notice whatever you can sense in that channel right now.

This is tasting.

So those are the first five channels of experience: touching, hearing, seeing, smelling and tasting. You have known them as the five senses ever since you first learnt about them at school.

See if you have the mental agility to switch your awareness between the channels at will. Spending a few seconds with each.

Touching.

Hearing.

Seeing.

Smelling.

Tasting.

Hearing.

Touching.

Seeing.

Touching.

Hearing.

Nice one.

Now to the sixth sense. This is not something mystical or special. Instead it is just a recognition that alongside all the experiences we receive through our physical senses, there are also these things called thoughts and moods. These are no more or less real than the five physical senses.

Being aware of the contents of our minds can be a little trickier than being aware of our physical senses and so that is why we work our way up first, developing the clarity and agility we need to keep up with our runaway thoughts and emotions.

So let's pay attention to the mind. Keeping the body and the face relaxed, just noticing how your mind is.

Notice how you know how to do that.

And notice what comes up.

There might be thoughts. There might be a particular mood, emotion or state of mind. There might be a sense of calm.

Just know what is here to be known. Know it clearly and without any agenda.

This is thinking.

This is how the mind is.

So that is the full range of what it is possible to be aware of. Touching, hearing, seeing, smelling, tasting and thinking.

There are two ways in which we can train in 'six-sense awareness'. The first is to deliberately switch between all the different channels of experience. So why don't you try doing that now, using the words here as a reminder of the channels and then moving your attention from one to another.

Touching, hearing, seeing, smelling, tasting and thinking.

The other, simpler way to train in six-sense awareness is to have the intention to be aware of everything and note which channels come up.

At any one time, one of the six channels will be most dominant. The practice therefore is to note whichever predominates and say the corresponding word to your-self – either internally or actually out loud. This is best done every one or two seconds or so.

For example, as I write this right now my experience is thinking, touching, touching, seeing, thinking, thinking, hearing, touching, touching.

Try it yourself now. Saying a word every couple of seconds that best captures what is most present for you. And if you're not sure what is present or what you're supposed to be doing, just say 'Confused' and try again in a few seconds' time once it has changed.

———

For many people this technique can be quite different to other styles of meditation they've done before. While it is actually based on a very traditional technique, it is the emphasis on saying words out loud which is a relatively recent invention. It can take a little getting used to, but one of its real advantages is how it can help maintain momentum. When we're starting out in mindfulness, it is often the case that we think we're following the instructions when in fact we have lost awareness. By keeping up a regular rhythm of noting, we have a 100 per cent guarantee that we are being aware of our experience, even if that awareness manifests simply as confusion. When we are able to honestly note what is happening every few seconds, not only is our awareness keen and bright, but we also build up flexibility as our mind jumps from experience to experience. This flexibility is especially valuable when looking to develop mindfulness in all parts of our life because we learn how to stay present and aware to all kinds of things. This technique does work if you only say the word internally to yourself but doing it out loud is more powerful. We are less likely to drift away when our task is actually saying a word rather than just thinking it. Obviously, the out-loud style does break our cover as invisible meditators, but it can be worth it.

———

Ten Meditations

Designed to help you be present in all kinds of places

 Tourist Mind

If you're anything like me, whenever I am visiting a new city or country, my attention is naturally brighter and I am more interested in everything around me. Buildings become more compelling. I notice more details in the people and shops, and it's so much easier to be present walking down the street because everything feels so alive and different. As much as we'd like to, we can't be on holiday all the time. But we can use our imagination and bring those qualities of mind to bear wherever we are, adding brightness and interest and presence to what can be experienced as our humdrum, everyday surroundings. This practice invites us to pretend to be a tourist in the places we think we already know so well. So while I don't necessarily advise donning the sunglasses and Bermuda shorts, I suggest you take on the tourist mind. Looking at everything through the eyes of a tourist – with the freshness, interest and even naivety it can involve. The simplest way to do this is to look for a detail in a street or building or train station that you have not noticed before and encourage a sense of interest or curiosity around it.

Stop Sign

As I've said before, one of the main challenges of making mobile mindfulness real is remembering to practise it in the first place. To solve this problem we need to create triggers and signs around the places where we spend the most time. These triggers will remind us to be present. Fortunately, our world is already full of signs so all we need to do is reframe them for developing our mindfulness. If you spend a lot of time walking or travelling, then stop signs are among some of the most convenient. Every time you see a sign asking us to stop (a traffic light, for instance) then do so. Red lights and bus stops become blessings when we use them as reminders to turn inside, re-establish awareness and check in with our senses and our mood. Traffic lights and bus stops are the most common signage that we'll see when we're out and about in an urban landscape but we can also use whatever symbol we want. Exit signs on motorways or in buildings become invitations to let go of negative thinking. Street names are reminders to drop our attention into our feet. Feel free to be playful and work out your own, charging up seemingly ordinary signs with whatever mindfulness meaning feels most appropriate to you. Let your landscape become a playground for your self-awareness.

Weather Face

Our face is one of the most sensitive parts of our body but it is underused as a meditation object. This technique uses the sensations we feel on our face while walking to encourage presence. All we need to do is feel the wind on our face or notice a subtle temperature difference across the face. People pay tens of thousands of pounds to get their hands on a convertible car, just so they can drive around the countryside feeling the wind through their hair. If only they knew that you can achieve that feeling for free just by putting your awareness into your face and head. Even five seconds of feeling the weather on our face can be enough to refresh us on a busy, stressful day. It is like taking a tiny holiday from what had been on our mind just before. We often use the same language to describe our moods as we do the weather, so this technique helps bring a bit more calm and softness to our experience instead of bracing ourselves against things by being so tight all the time. It also has the added advantage of encouraging us to be in an open and receiving mode. Unlike other techniques, such as breath-based concentration where we actively look for our meditation object, here we sit back and let whatever happens happen, our face acting like a satellite receiver for simple physical sensation. This shows us that we can be fully aware of our experience and remain bright and alert but at the same time entirely relaxed and open.

Full Breakfast

Mindfulness and food should be really good friends since for many of us, our mealtimes can be the most sensual times of the day. But despite that, we can often wolf down our food while our attention is on something else entirely, thereby missing out on much of the pleasure of the experience. This is a bit of a shame since there aren't too many other moments which have the potential for such simple pleasure. Breakfast is the best meal to start with since it can help set our intention not only for other mealtimes but for the whole of the day. As much as you'd like to eat breakfast on the hoof or catch up with the news or even skip breakfast entirely, every once in a while try sitting down to your first meal of the day with no other distractions. Without making it too much like a weird ritual, pay as much attention as you can to the experience of eating – the flavours, the smells, the textures and the movements of your face and jaw. If you're able to, you can even notice the more subtle movements of the mind such as expectation and wanting. When you first try this exercise, our habit of hurrying to get on with the day will still be quite strong and so just notice when that rushing habit shows up and see if you can avoid the need to give into it. Doing this once or twice a week can make a big difference. As a keen cook myself, I know that whoever made the food will definitely be pleased that you're appreciating their efforts a little bit more.

 I See People

The idea of this exercise is simply to see people as they are, but please don't be deceived by how outrageously simple this sounds. When we look at people, whether they are just other passengers in the same train carriage or people walking down the street, we tend to layer stories all over them. We make judgements. We consider them attractive or unattractive. We make up entire narratives based on the tiniest amount of information in the tiniest amount of time. Instead, the invitation here is to see people just as they are, without the filters of our views and opinions. We do that by bringing an open attention to anyone we see throughout the day and making the intention to see them in detail but without judgement. And whenever we notice our minds creating some kind of judgement or story, we should choose instead to let that go and use that as a cue to reconnect with what we can actually see. Sometimes we will see joy in people. Sometimes we will see tension. Sometimes we will see nothing much at all. Watch the tendency of the mind to create stories and when a story arises let mindfulness redirect you to whatever is actually there. Remember of course not to stare since that can get kind of creepy.

Emotional Web

Cat pictures. Double rainbows. News stories reminding us of everyday injustices that take place all around us. The internet is full of things that get us going, creating reactions that run the full range of the emotional spectrum. The 'emotional web' technique helps us avoid all of our attention getting stuck in whichever screen we are using. Instead we learn to be aware of the reactions to the content that we see. There are few better times to watch how we react than when we are surfing the web. Pay attention to how your body and mind react when you come across your favourite websites. Notice how you get drawn into some stories and pictures and not into others. Watch how boredom arises as you read an article and start looking for something else. Watch your heart open when you come across an uplifting story. Notice what your reaction is to yet more difficult news coming from conflict-ravaged parts of our world. Don't just surf. Watch the surfing and watch it well. There is a lot to be learnt.

Inbox Addict

Addiction is a strong word but there definitely have been times when I've felt pretty close to addiction when it comes to checking my email and my social network feeds. I'd do it first thing in the morning when barely even awake. I'd do it while having dinner with my wife. I'd do it dozens of times a day, seemingly outside of my control. What changed my relationship with it all was turning it into a meditation technique. The first part of the technique is simply to know when it is happening. Sometimes you only notice it when your hand has already reached for your device and is scrolling down the feed. Other times you catch it earlier in the process, and as you get better at noticing it, you might even catch it just as a twitch in the hand. Once you've become more aware of the whole process of going to check your messages, the second part of the technique is noticing if any particular emotion or feeling precedes the movement at all. For me it was noticing that there was a strong correlation between when I was feeling bored or lonely and when I checked my phone. When you are able to notice that snippet of emotion and leave it as it is, just by having that level of awareness in that moment can cut out the habit of constant checking. This starts to short-circuit the need to fix the boredom or loneliness and you are able to let it fizzle itself out.

 ## Signal Bars

Our ability to communicate with others, whether by phone or via the internet, is dependent on how good our connection is. And thanks to phone displays, the way we measure that connection or signal is by bars. If there is only a very weak signal, then there is one bar, and there are five full bars if our signal is as good as it gets. On the occasions when we are hidden in an underground bunker or we are in the remote countryside we may have no signal at all. The idea of this simple and playful technique is to use the idea of signal bars as a metaphor for the quality of connection with other people. So when you are next in a conversation with someone, check in with how connected you really are with them in that moment. Give yourself a rating based on one to five bars. Take care to just be honest with the level of your connection without adding any extra self-judgement on top for not having as many bars as you might have hoped. There is of course another option entirely. Sometimes, for whatever reason, you might just feel like you don't want to engage with anything or anyone around you. Maybe you are in that kind of mood or you are in a situation that you want to shut out such as finding yourself on a station platform full of overenergetic football fans. Do not feel like this is a failure, it just happens sometimes. If it does, simply note that you are in 'airplane mode'. Just be aware of the fact that if you do it when you are with friends, they might find it a little bit rude.

 Balanced Awareness

Sometimes we just don't feel like doing formal meditation. That's OK. It happens to everyone. All the time. It's pretty easy for us to come up with some compelling excuse not to sit. Regularity and momentum are absolutely key to getting the most out of mindfulness – break your rhythm at your peril. Just don't beat yourself up about it, since that will only add another layer of self-criticism and we have quite enough of that already. The other strategy is just to sit down and meditate anyway. This is often the best way forward since it will show us that our excuses are just as untrue as any of our other thoughts, and it's very rare indeed that you'll ever regret doing a session of formal meditation. Balanced awareness is an important technique and is best started by taking a comfortable seated posture. With eyes open or closed, the instruction is simply to just watch what happens. Different aspects of experience will come into your awareness: sounds, thoughts, physical sensations, and all the rest. When possible, just watch them come and go, being fully aware of everything that happens but making no distinction between one thing or another. While doing this you will notice that there are some things for which it is not possible to maintain this position of balance. Your mind will go out to meet things, start judging them, make stories about them or get involved. The key is to simply notice and see if there are any patterns that you can observe. Which patterns make it possible to maintain balance and which don't? This practice works best if you can do it for at least twenty minutes. If this feels too long for you, then why not include your sense of impatience and restlessness as just another part of your experience?

Time Travel

One of my favourite ways to make my formal meditation sessions last that little bit longer is what I call my 'three strikes and out policy' and it is most useful when you're not using a timer. Whenever the thought comes up that you should probably end your meditation now that counts as one strike and the idea is to only stop after that has happened three times. What might surprise you is that there can be quite a big gap between the strikes, again showing us how lightweight our thoughts can be. This technique is called 'time travel' and is a variant of this chapter's core noting practice, and while best tried initially as a formal practice, once you've got the hang of it, it can then be taken out and about with you in your back pocket. While sitting comfortably, make the intention to watch your thoughts, resting your attention in whatever way makes most sense for you in order to observe your thoughts as they come and go. Then when thoughts arise, notice if they are related to the 'past', the 'present' or the 'future' by simply saying the word either out loud or silently to yourself. There will be periods of time when no thoughts will arise at all and all that is present is the intention to be aware and the bright awareness that comes with that intention. When that is the case you can simply note 'present' since that is what you are in those moments. Do this practice for about ten minutes and at the end review what time zones your mind spent most time travelling to.

When thoughts arise, notice if they are related to the 'past', the 'present' or the 'future' by simply saying the word either out loud or silently to yourself.

Chapter 5
This is Coping

Be warned. This chapter contains the secret of mindfulness.

Kirsten Schultz is a spoonie. She has two chronic pain conditions. One is systemic juvenile rheumatoid arthritis and the other is fibromyalgia. Both mean that she suffers some kind of pain in her joints at all times as well as regular episodes when parts of her body flare up and the pain becomes even more severe. Now in her twenties, Kirsten has had chronic pain since she was five years old. I first came across her while obsessively checking Twitter for mentions of one of our apps and noticed how she had posted quite a few times on how useful she was finding it. A quick google stalk showed me that Kirsten was a very active blogger in the 'spoonie' community, with spoonie being a name that people with a variety of chronic pain and chronic fatigue syndromes call themselves.

One of the downsides of making apps is that you only rarely get the chance to meet the people in person whose lives have benefitted from your work. Writing this book was a wonderful opportunity because I had to speak with people to get their stories and it was a genuine pleasure to make contact with them, and especially Kirsten. She is a seriously impressive human being and when we spoke, I found her story to be both inspiring and instructive.

Kirsten had heard about the benefits of yoga and meditation in a magazine while still in school, and although she had tried and enjoyed both at that early age the rest of life got in the way and they fell by the wayside. Then a few years ago a close friend in the spoonie community died and she noticed that she was at risk of falling into a downward spiral. She had pain, and she had anger about having pain, and now on top of all that she was grieving and afraid. So she decided to restart her interest in mindfulness and meditation using an app to help her practise.

When you have chronic pain, to make progress you have to realise that there is the pain itself and then there is my reaction to that pain. Before mindfulness, my default reaction was anger. I was angry at the pain and also at myself. And alongside all that anger, there was anxiety and all the self-criticism as I struggled to process what I was going through. The pain is painful but it is the fear, the anger, the upset and the anxiety that drag you down. Meditation helps me find my centre. It helps me reduce the negative reaction to the pain because out of everything that is the most difficult part.

I take my medication and that helps soften the pain itself. But it is the meditation, together with the therapy that I do, that helps me deal with the anger and the reactions. I am now able to focus on the sensations instead of the emotions. Separating out the anxiety from the pain has made all the difference. Sometimes it's easy to figure out which one sets the other off but sometimes it's not so clear. Mindfulness isn't necessarily so helpful for that and that's where the therapy can be really useful.

Mindfulness also shows me that even the hardest pain or the most difficult emotion is just a temporary thing. Noticing that change has made a massive difference. The pain is still there but now I can even be grateful for it. I now have the self-awareness to notice any discomfort and itching before it becomes full-blown pain. That's quite a change from when all I could do was be angry and resentful.

When I asked Kirsten about whether her mindfulness practice has leaked out into parts of her life other than working with her chronic pain, she lit up even more.

Aside from being more peaceful in general, the main difference has to be in my relationships. Mindfulness has really helped improve my relationships which previously had been quite difficult. I guess that working on being compassionate to myself means that I'm able to be more compassionate to others. That's also how I see all the blogging I do. Sharing my own story and struggles with others through blogging and other social media is an expression of my compassion. It's part of my practice.

I've met a lot of mindfulness experts in my time. But as she is someone who has lived with pain for the majority of her life, I've never heard as clear or as real an articulation of how mindfulness helps us transform our experience of the difficult as the one Kirsten shared with me.

Some of you will recognise bits of Kirsten's story in yourself. So many people have some kind of condition, be that a physical one like hers or a more mental one such as anxiety or depression. Those of you that do will know that irrespective of whether the initial pain is physical or mental, so much of the challenge is working with all the negative thinking that comes up. Physical pain is hard and whether we have it or not, it is often still the emotional and mental pain which is the most difficult to bear.

Some of you might find Kirsten's story quite unlike your own experience and the idea of having to deal with pain on a daily basis feels very different to what your life is like. It may even make you think that you have nothing to complain about given how tough her experience sounds. However, it is important to recognise that we all know pain. We all have our own experience of both physical and emotional pain. At the time of writing this chapter I was experiencing physical tension in my neck and upper back at a level of severity that I'd not had before. I did notice after speaking to Kirsten that finding out more about her story and her experience definitely put my own relatively minor physical difficulty into a bigger perspective. But it didn't stop it from being there and it didn't stop it from being something I had to deal with.

We all know pain. We all know what it is to face the difficult. For some of us it might be chronic pain or anxiety or depression. For others it will be more like grief or illness, heartbreak or loneliness. It can be physical, emotional and everything in between. It can be a shared pain or something very personal.

This chapter is for you.

It is for the you who lives through painful times.

That might be right now. Or it might be later on when

life takes a turn for the worse. And as much as we'd like to ignore it, deep down we know that those times *will* come.

So let's do this.

Come close and listen even closer, I'm about to tell you the secret of mindfulness. Kirsten knows it and it's about time you did too. OK. Are you ready? Here it is.

The more personally we take life, the worse a time we have. When we learn to hold life that bit more lightly, the happier we are. And mindfulness builds our ability to do that.

That's it.

Done.

You're welcome.

OK, let's try something to explain this a little more. Take this book and, without causing yourself any pain, really strengthen your grip on it so that you are holding it as tightly as you possibly can while still reading it. At this moment there are two things happening: the reading itself and the tension with which we are holding it. While we are holding the book tightly, the tension gets in the way of us getting the most out of the words. Feel what this is like. Know this.

Now relax your hands back to normal and feel that difference and that relief.

You are still reading the book but now you are just holding it more lightly. The book is still here. Life is still here. But now the relationship is one of freedom and lightness. Notice what that feels like.

Then remember how Kirsten explained how mindfulness worked for her. She said that first there is the pain, the basic physical sensations, and then there is her reaction to the pain, such as anger or resentment, layered on top. So there are two layers: the first is basic experience and the second is how we relate or react to it. Thanks to her mindfulness training, she was able to see that and through that seeing she then went on to relax that reaction so that it became not one of anger or frustration but one of allowing. That is quite a change. The basic sensations of pain don't necessarily go away but her relationship with it has been transformed. In her case, it even transformed into gratitude.

Another way to describe it is that much of the suffering we endure in difficult times is down to our struggling and fighting with what is happening. Soften that struggle, soften that fight and everything changes. That is the secret. However, knowing it as an idea is all very well but it only becomes real for us when we see it directly for ourselves. That's where the practice comes in.

What has that got to do with taking things personally? When we strip everything back, the most fundamental mechanic of how mindfulness works is by allowing us to observe or be aware of something, something which we originally thought of as being part of ourselves, and seeing it as an external object. Because if we can see it, it can't be us.

That might be a little bit too abstract and technical so let me put it another way. I am feeling angry. By paying attention to what is happening, I can see anger as an experience. This will probably manifest as heat and tension in the body alongside a maelstrom of angry thoughts. The experience moves from being *I am angry* to *there is anger*. This is the movement of taking something personal and making it an object which can be known. This simple act creates that small but precious amount of space which is the difference between just acting blindly out of anger or having a moment to compose ourselves and see things a little bit more clearly.

This movement from something that is part of us to something that is out there is what I mean by not taking life so personally. When we look at it in this way we can see that it's the same basic mechanic as in therapy, going for a cup of tea with a friend or the practice of writing down our experiences in a journal. By talking a problem through, or writing it down, we move something which we have been holding very closely outside of ourselves, changing the relationship in the process. Mindfulness follows the same principle. Through our awareness, a thing inside becomes a thing outside and the result is relief.

We can't always change what life throws up for us, but we *can* change how we relate to it. A family member dies. A friend falls very ill. A relationship ends. Work pressures get so bad that just seeing that we've got an email from a particular colleague makes us want to throw up. This is just what happens. I know it and you know it too. The invitation of mindfulness is not to grin and bear it like a stone statue. That is madness. The invitation is to meet life as it is and let our relationship with life be one of lightness and balance instead of tension and struggle. Because that is something which we can have a say in.

This must also include our relationship with ourselves. This is a chapter about coping with difficult experience and so now it is time to turn to a difficult experience which is all too rarely spoken about. Yes. It's time to talk about the voices in our head.

I'm never going to get this done.

No one is going to buy the book let alone read it.

It's not even any good. Why did you ever think you could write this thing in the first place?

I'm not going to have any time to get it to where I want it to be.

The other mindfulness books that come out at the same time as this one are going to be so much better.

Stop trying to be funny.

Who am I to be doing this?

Why am I doing this again?

It's useless. I'm useless. Everything is useless.

I think it's time I got a proper job.

That is just the edited highlights of some of the voices which piped up while writing this chapter. I could have gone on but I think you get the point.

Whether you call it inner commentary, the inner critic, negative self-talk, the voices in our head that are always giving us a hard time, we all know what we're talking about. It's an everyday part of life for the vast majority of us and it's time to start letting it go.

It is now known that our brain has a tendency towards the negative. When there is both a good and a bad side to a story then more often than not this negative bias means that we will prioritise the bad. It is therefore little wonder that our minds have over the years become filled with guilt, regret, self-judgement, doubt and all the rest. This is just

We can't always change what life throws up for us, but we can change how we relate to it.

what it is to be human. Inner commentary is perhaps ultimately a part of ourselves that was genuinely on our side but over time has lost its way and is now just more hindrance than help.

When I searched on Amazon for how many books there were with 'happiness' in the title, the number I got was 43,806. That's a lot of words. While I'm sure many of those writers are much more qualified than I am, if you *were* to ask me how to be happy, I would say this: make friends with your inner commentary and don't let what it says dictate your life.

The same principles apply to all the negative inner commentary relating to dealing with pain. See it. Acknowledge it. Relax around it. Let it go. This is a life-long practice but we can see results surprisingly quickly. I've met many people who have learnt mindfulness through clinical referrals to help them deal with really difficult conditions like anxiety or chronic fatigue syndrome. If I ask them if they could boil down everything they have learnt, what would it be, the most common reply is not a particular technique or exercise but that *thoughts are not facts*. So many of us completely buy into the idea that all the negative thoughts that we have are actually true, and are often even unaware that that is what is happening. Mindfulness helps us start to shine a light on how our doubt and self-criticism are not as real as we first thought. That is so important since it is where transformation and freedom can be found.

Something that I have found personally very useful when dealing with the difficult is the idea of layers. The first layer is the basic pain, be it physical or emotional. Then as we've already seen, on top of that is the second layer of how we relate to that first layer. What happens then is that we can also have a reaction to that second layer and all of a sudden we have constructed a whole tower of trouble. Here's an example of what I mean. *There is some pain in my neck and shoulders*. That's the first basic layer. *I don't like this pain*. That is layer two and makes the area around the pain even more tense. *Why am I even complaining about this pain when there are people in the world who have to deal with real pain?* This is layer three and is the first emotional layer, made up of good old-fashioned guilt as I start judging myself. *I am such a selfish person and I'm now going to remind myself of all the times I've been really selfish by making a big list of them and replaying them over and over in my mind*. Layer four now sees the inner commentator in full flow and this pattern of self-judgement and emotional pain has become the most prominent part of the experience, with that initial pain pushed into the background by all the negative self-referential stories.

The same thing can happen with an emotion. *I'm not sure why but I feel a bit sad*. This could just be for no particular reason but it is all that's needed to start building. *I'm such a sad person*. The second layer sees me relate to the little feeling of sadness by fully identifying with it. *It is always going to be like this. I am always going to be sad.* The third layer then turns a moment of sadness into a fixed permanent state. *I am so useless.* The fourth layer then relates to that sense of fixed sadness with negative self-judgement. While this can all happen in a blink of an eye, mindfulness allows us the space and the ability to step outside of it so that we can see the process happen. Not only does seeing it happen reduce its power, just being able to see basic sensations as they are enables us to meet the difficult with balance and poise instead of anguish and struggle. All of which means that we can stop the process before it even gets going.

In the long run this is an effective and sustainable way of dealing with difficult experiences when they arise. I've often heard it said that another good mindfulness practice for tough times is to say to ourselves that 'this too will pass'. Affirmations like this can be helpful but what is ultimately the most transformative is not just to remind ourselves that things change but to see the change. When we notice that a difficult experience has ended, even if just for a moment we are able to really clock the absence of the difficult, our mind becomes more familiar with the knowledge that even the toughest times do come to an end. We then start to undermine the idea that *things are always going to be like this* because deep inside ourselves we know that nothing stays the same.

At this point it is only right to put in a couple of caveats with regard to using mindfulness as a way of coping with the difficult. The first is, I hope, obvious. If you have been diagnosed with an actual clinical condition or suspect you may have one, the first port of call should always be your doctor.

Clinical mental health issues are common and while everyone suffers from some kind of inner turmoil, if it is on the more serious end of the spectrum, it should be looked at professionally. Mindfulness does have a lot to bring to the domain of mental health but it is not a panacea.

My second caveat is perhaps less obvious. The instructions of this chapter invite us to directly look at difficult experiences we are having and then start to relax our relationship towards them as the route to relief. Sometimes this will not be possible because what we are looking at is just too difficult and we don't yet have the balance or stability the task demands. What's more, paying attention to something can by definition make that thing more prominent and so we might find that there is actually more pain or more negativity than we first thought. Seeing that is pretty good from an awareness perspective but not so helpful if it's actually quite tough. So my recommendation is to be gentle with yourself. If working with difficult experience is too challenging, then try another tactic. Mindfulness is made up of a whole family of techniques and part of the skill of a meditator is knowing which one to use at which time. Sometimes we can look the difficult directly in the face and other times we need to play the relaxation card, moving our attention somewhere more tolerable. This is not a failure; it is wisdom. Never criticise yourself for having to duck out if you need to. That just lays more self-judgement on top of what is happening and, to be honest, we've already got quite enough of that.

———

Know your mind, relax the fight
Core technique #4: Knowing your attitude

Working with the more challenging parts of our inner lives is not always easy. As we've already said, looking at the difficult means that it becomes even more magnified because we're putting so much attention on it. That is why getting our relaxation and focus on is always the best place to start.

You know how to do this now. Know the feelings of holding the book. Check in with your posture.

Let the body be relaxed. Pay particular care to relaxing the face, the jaw and any of your signature areas.

We've already seen how at any one time there are two things going on: our direct sensory experience and our relationship to that experience. How we meet experience matters. But far too often we just aren't aware of how we are relating to or meeting things, despite how massive an effect that has on our lives. So the whole point of this technique is to bring that into awareness and see what happens.

It uses two questions. The first is, *what is happening?* This, as you now know, brings us into presence and primes the mind to be alert. The second question comes in a few versions so you should just choose whichever one makes most sense to you. *How am I relating to what is happening? What is my attitude? What am I layering on top of this? What am I bringing to this?* Or my personal favourite, *how am I meeting this?*

There are four ways in which we can meet experience. The most obvious one is that we push it away, trying to get rid of it. Then there is the opposite: we grab on to it, wanting it to keep going. The third way we meet experience is to ignore it. We deny it's happening at all and so we look elsewhere, turning a blind eye.

The fourth and final way is balance. When faced with a difficult experience, we let it be as it is, without adding anything else on. That's what we're going to give a go.

When what is happening is relatively neutral, such as the touch of this book or the feeling of our feet on the ground, it's pretty easy to keep the mind balanced. Notice that. Ask yourself what holding the book feels like and know that experience of simply touching. Then check if you are meeting that experience in a particular way or bringing anything additional to it. Given that it's a neutral sensation, what's most likely is that there isn't much at all.

It becomes more challenging when what is happening is hard to bear. Looking at the difficult is difficult and so if it ever becomes too much, please just acknowledge that, stop and move your attention back to something more neutral. There absolutely are times when the best tactic is to run away. Fight and flight are both legitimate strategies and so you should only do as much as feels OK for you.

With that disclaimer, let's move our attention to the body. Find a part of your body which feels uncomfortable. That may be quite obvious or it may be quite subtle. Either is fine so just take your time. As I write in this moment, for me it is a big knot of tension in the upper left side of my neck. What is it for you? It might not be a clear physical pain and instead be an emotional or mental difficulty. Tune into whatever it is for you right now.

How are you meeting it?

Can you relax any of the resistance to that tension?

In my own case I am aware of two different things: the painful sensation in my neck and also how I'm trying to resist that through other areas of my body being tight as well. My breath, my face, the wider area of the neck, all those areas are tight as well as if fighting the neck pain. So I deliberately relax them.

What resistance do you notice and can you relax any of it?

And notice what happens when you do. Does it change the intensity of the overall experience?

What you might notice is that when you meet tension with clear seeing and balance, it actually becomes less prominent.

Now move the mind away from any tension and just let it be a bit more freestyle. Still being present and knowing what is happening.

And every now and then just asking that all important question, *how am I meeting this?*

Know experience. Notice if there is any struggle. Relax that struggle.

See how that changes your experience.

———

Expectation can seem like a bit of a paradox when it comes to mindfulness. We come to the practice because we have something we want to deal with or get better at. But if we put too much pressure on getting instant results, then we add more tension to the mix and risk sabotaging our progress. This is where trust comes in.

Turning towards mindfulness is an act of kindness to ourselves. It is a statement that things can get better and that when lined up in the right way we have the inner resources to get there. Trust that.

We also have to trust in the process. Results will happen at their own pace and while it is a bit of a cliché that good things come to those who wait, there is also some truth in there. Do keep reviewing to see what changes are happening. Consistent practice does result in all sorts of different benefits and if we make sure we notice them as they come up, we will get the most mindfulness bang for our mindfulness buck.

Turning towards mindfulness is an act of kindness to ourselves. It is a statement that things can get better and that when lined up in the right way we have the inner resources to get there.

But review lightly. Progress in meditation is ultimately progress in our ability to let go and there are some times when letting go of the expectations of specific results is the very thing that allows them to happen.

———

Ten Meditations
Designed to deal with the difficult wherever we are

⚡ Hello Monsters

I don't know if you've watched much *Doctor Who* but if you have, you will know that there is something special about naming monsters. The good doctor will only be able to work out his plan to get rid of the monster that is plaguing that particular forty-five-minute show once he has worked out what its name is. There is a moment when he names the monster out loud and in the very doing, it somehow loses a little bit of power. This is a thing that can actually happen when we are faced with our own inner monsters. When you have any challenging thoughts rampaging through your mind, try naming them and saying hello. *Hello, anxiety. Hello, guilt. Why, hello there, Mr Sense-Of-Feeling-Worthless. So lovely to see you again!* Doing this can not only externalise the experience but it can also puncture its power due to the lightness of it all. To add even more effectiveness, say hello to those monsters aloud if you can. Once you've named them you will be much quicker at noticing when they come back, and taking this light-hearted approach means that we can begin to welcome them with friendliness instead of aversion.

⚡ Drop It

This is one of the first ever meditation techniques that I designed for myself. So the fact that I still use it over ten years later on a pretty much daily basis must mean either that it's pretty good or that I haven't moved on at all. I like to think it's the former. It's actually based on an old and probably made-up traditional meditation story. A student is carrying two big pots for the teacher. The teacher points to one of the pots and shouts out for the student to, 'Drop it!' The student duly complies and the pot clatters to the ground. The teacher then points to the other pot and shouts, 'Drop it!' The same thing happens again. The teacher then points straight at the student's head and shouts, 'Drop it!' This story inspired me to try doing the same thing. Whatever the activity, whenever I notice any negative thinking about myself during the day I just say 'Drop it!' to myself, and often out loud. What those magic two words do is simply deflate the energy of the self-criticism, resulting in it not having enough power for me to then buy into the storyline it's trying to present. What's even lovelier is that when you make this technique a habit it sort of starts to do it by itself, nipping negativity in the bud sometimes even before you notice that it is there.

 Seeing Nature

Spending time in the countryside can be just what we need to get a bigger perspective on things. The detail of trees, flowers and wildlife can remind us of different rhythms and the often vast views and spaces the countryside contains can naturally encourage our minds into a wider sense of awareness and relaxation than we are typically used to. This can feel very far away when we're caught up in the constriction of urban life and so a simple way to remind us of that is to see nature where we can. The most obvious way to do that is to spend a short time experiencing a park or green space but that too is not possible for many of us much of the time. A good way to see nature is to notice a houseplant or a single tree or a bird or even an insect and allow yourself a few moments to see it as a part of nature. And the simplest way is to just look up at the sky for a moment and let the sense of that immense space dilute whatever is in your mind at the time.

The Mindful Troll

One of the best ways to hone our skills in relaxing the judgement of ourselves is by relaxing our judgement of others. This is a technique that is unusual and strangely fun in equal measure and we start by going to the website of a news outlet that you know is on the complete other side of the opinion spectrum to you. So if you're a bit left-wing then choose a right-wing paper and vice versa. Then type in a contentious topic in that little search bar and bring up an article that effectively represents all you think is bad when it comes to human opinion. Then just watch your mind as you read it. See if you can notice the difference between reading the article and the reaction that comes up. And when you notice very strong negative thoughts appearing about how idiotic the writer is and how angry you're becoming see if you can observe those thoughts just as they are, without overlaying anything on top of them. Let the thoughts and judgement just be the natural result of what you're reading, nothing more and nothing less than that. When done in a light-hearted way this technique can be quite an education into how reactive our minds can actually be.

 RAIN

I don't normally go for acronym meditations, which is where there is some word like 'SPACE' or 'STOP' or 'BREATHE' and then we have to learn a contrived set of stages which correspond to each letter in the word. But I'm including RAIN here since it's the best of this kind of meditation by far and so many people have found it to be a lifesaver when it all gets a bit too much. The way it works is by you simply going through each of the four stages in turn and in doing so, you will find some space from that which feels just too much to bear. The first stage is *Recognise*. This is basic mindfulness, recognising what it is that's happening, not what you think is happening. The next stage is *Allow*. Even though it is hard, is there something in you that can just let what is happening happen? The third stage is *Investigate*. What else can you discover about the experience? Are there any more details to notice or any other sensations happening at the same time? The final stage is *Not Me*. Are you able to see that by observing the difficulty, it is not a part of you? Those are the four stages and we do whichever of them we can, even if it's just the first. That's RAIN and when remembered, it can put out some serious fires.

⚡ Hold On

There are two overall type of mindfulness strategy when dealing with difficult emotions or experiences. The majority of this chapter is all about seeing what is happening for what it is and relaxing our relationship with it. This is ultimately the most powerful way forward but there are times when we just can't do it. These are the times when we have to take the other route, which is to place our mind somewhere else. This is not a cop-out. It is just being skilful and knowing what is right for us at the right time. So when it is too much, try this technique of literally finding something to hold on to. Find whatever you can. It could be a table. It could be a wall. It could be yourself. Wrap your hands and, if you need to, your arms around whatever you can. What makes it mindfulness is that you then try your absolute best to put your mind into the felt physical sensations in your hands. In the turmoil of that moment you have found something to hold on to so you put your mind there. Even if you can do it for a moment, that is one moment when you are out of the storm. Over time you'll get better at doing this and your body awareness will become a life raft.

 Whack-a-Thought

I've had my fair share of obsessive thought patterns – chatter and thinking that will just keep coming up again and again – and it's when going to bed that I find them the most disruptive. Even when I tried using all the tactics I know, they would still pop up, as if laughing at me and keeping me awake. Then I noticed something very interesting. If I expected those thoughts to come up and lay in wait for them, that very priming of my mind would make them less likely to appear. And when they did, I would be ready, recognising their arrival so quickly that they lost much of their power very rapidly indeed. It's like standing by an animal's hole waiting for it to pop out. We just whack it over its head with the strength of our awareness, like the whack-a-mole or splat-a-rat games of old-school amusement arcades. I've since seen that it works for any type of thought at all. So as a way to shortcut yourself into a quiet mind, just place all your attention on your mind, waiting to see what thoughts come up and clocking them when they do. You might be surprised by what happens.

 Back Hand

This is another manual meditation. When we say that we know something like the back of our hand, it means that we know it inside out. But when I looked at the back of my hand, I realised that this couldn't be further from the truth. Something I often do when I'm having a difficult time is try and get back in touch with a sense of wonder. One way of doing this is to take a much bigger perspective but that can be hard to do when our mind is constricted and contracted by worry and negativity. This technique therefore takes the opposite approach and keeps our mind in its narrow state but uses that narrowness to look at things in a different way. And what we do is simply look at the back of our hand in extreme close-up. Look at it in as much detail as you can. The pattern of tiny triangles that make up the skin. How those triangles vary in size across different parts of the hand. Look at how the little hairs are thicker at the point they come out of the skin and then taper to a bit of a point. Notice the variation in colour across different parts of the hand. Notice the variation in the density of hairs. While you are doing this, some thoughts of self-judgement come up, about what your hand is like and what this exercise is like. Notice how different it is to hear those thoughts compared to the simplicity of paying attention to the detail of your hand. When looking at your hand, see if you can also get in touch with a sense of wonder at how extraordinary it is. In all the turmoil that life brings, it can be hard to remember that we are still full of beauty and mystery. So if we need to do a little hack like this to get in touch with that, then so be it.

Thought Gaps

A good way to start a formal sitting meditation is to remember why you are doing it. Even if done for a few seconds this can really help us connect with our intention to look after ourselves and others, thus setting a lovely tone to our overall session. Having a clear sense of intention is particularly useful for this technique, which is one of the more subtle and tricksy ones, but like most of the formal practices and core techniques in the book once you get the hang of it, you can then go ahead and take it mobile. It can comprise a whole session in itself or be something you tag on after something like a body scan when the mind is relatively quiet. Pay attention to the gaps between thoughts. That's it. Even if the mind is full of thinking, there will be times when it's not. Just know that in as direct and unmediated a way as possible. Just as there are gaps between letters, words, paragraphs and lines here in this book, there are gaps in our thoughts but our minds tend to get drawn to the content instead of the space. Another way of putting it is to pay attention to the background rather than the foreground. When we notice the gaps in this way we see that thoughts are not permanent things. When we see it once it can give us some relief and calm, even if only for a millisecond. When we see it over and over again, the idea becomes imprinted that underneath all the noise, the mind is fundamentally a quiet, peaceful place. When that does become imprinted, even when we are caught up, part of us will always know that the difficult is not the be all and end all. For me this has been one of the most valuable gifts of mindfulness.

Sound Bathing

It can be helpful to have a regular place where we do our formal practice. There is a little bit of a ritual element to always sitting in the same spot which can help our mind settle into meditation relatively quickly. There is also a real value to dedicating some time to sitting meditation at the times when life feels just that little bit too much. Just that act of making even a few minutes for stillness and self-care is one of the most generous things we can do for ourselves. But when the sensations feel too strong and the negative thinking relentless, even the tiniest amount of space is hard to find. This is the perfect time to lean the mind back into sound. This technique is perhaps most effective either when sitting in a formal meditation posture or when lying down before bedtime. But like so many of the meditations in this book, it really works anywhere. I'd also recommend trying it in the bath if you have one. With your eyes closed, put as much attention as you can afford into the overall sound of hearing. Because hearing is such an open sense, it encourages our mind to be open as well. Listen to sounds without the need to judge them or give them any meaning. Let sounds come and let them go, enjoying any spaciousness that comes about as a result. When our mind gets caught up in a thought or another sensation then just notice how different that is from the sense of spaciousness that you may have just experienced and open back out into the sense of hearing. If you can, treat a thought in the same way you'd treat a sound, letting it come up into awareness, do its thing, and then just fall back into silence. If you are trying this technique in the bath, you can think of these thoughts as being like bubbles.

Chapter 6
This is Connection

Dealing with ourselves is hard enough. Then there are other people.

Up to this point, we have primarily been using mindfulness to help us connect with ourselves. We've seen how we can become closer to our bodies, more present to what is happening and more allowing of our thoughts and emotions. Now it is time to turn our attention to connecting with others.

As our understanding and practice of mindfulness develop and mature and we become more stable and balanced, our care and our attention naturally expand to include other people. Our increased sensitivity to how our own mind and moods work shows us how our own wellbeing can be affected by those around us. The relationship between this thing we call ourselves and the people out there then starts to become of real interest.

Moving mindfulness from being an exclusively single-player game to a multiplayer game is an important shift. I'm generally a pretty calm chap but one of the things that does frustrate me is stock photography of meditation because it perpetuates all the kinds of stereotypes that hold it back. One of those stereotypes is that it is an activity that we do by ourselves. Do a Google image search of meditation and you'll see what I mean. Most of the images are of people in romantic natural locations, which look nothing like where we actually might be, and to boot, they are all by themselves. This is what I call the 'myth of the solo hero meditator'. We have this idea of a person on a mountaintop or in an idyllic forest practising in splendid isolation.

Images like this mean we end up becoming imprinted with the idea that meditation practice doesn't include other people. This is exacerbated not only by the emphasis on formal eyes-closed practice but also by the growth of single-player mindfulness apps, through which people primarily learn meditation by themselves. This is in stark contrast to the past where people mostly learnt it as part of a group class or with a teacher face to face.

All this means that even though there can be a natural outwards movement as our mindfulness grows, it can need some encouragement. Just because we are really good at one-player meditation does not always mean that we automatically play well with others. I've met lots of people in my time who are great solo meditators but don't always have the best social skills. By developing a sense of connection with others, we gain a wider perspective and are less likely to be obsessed with the minutiae of our own personal stories. It can also help soften any feelings of isolation or loneliness that are so quietly corrosive in today's world. A recent survey

By developing a sense of connection with others, we gain a wider perspective and are less likely to be obsessed with the minutiae of our own personal stories.

of London residents found that almost one in three people felt alone despite the enormous number of people around them. That's a big deal.

I came face to face with my own limitations as a solo meditator when I decided to try internet dating.

It was way back in 2008 when internet dating was not as pervasive as it is now. So unlike today there was still a little bit of a stigma around the idea of putting yourself out there and some of my friends, while fascinated by the whole idea, were terrified to do it themselves. I, however, had no such qualms. I had nothing to lose and felt full of adventure. Thus, I entered the fray with an open mind. Or so I thought.

One of the best things about training in mindfulness is that you become aware of so much more of yourself than ever before. Having done a fair bit of meditation before this point – both broad and deep – I thought I was a pretty balanced and together kind of person. And definitely not judgemental at all. Oh, whatever hubris. One of the *worst* things about training in mindfulness is that you become aware of so much more of yourself than ever before. And not all of it is particularly pretty. Those of you who know a little bit about the make-up of the brain will know that right down in the foundations of it all there is what's called the reptilian brain stem. So while we can have our angelic moments, we are still animals.

When I started internet dating the thing I noticed first was just how judgemental I actually was. *I have to filter out everyone taller than me. Let's make sure they have a certain type of education.* And no doubt I had some other criteria that I either conveniently cannot remember right now or am too embarrassed to share in public. Just setting up the search conditions, I noticed the voice that was very certain about the requirements I was looking for. Then on top of that there was the voice that was judging me for being so narrow-minded. It was quite a show. At least that's what I thought, because once the search was completed and all the profiles appeared, that's when the real show began.

Skimming over all the various pictures, I was able to see just how quick to judge I really was. *Not good-looking enough. Too quirky. Too much make-up.* And all the rest. Going into internet dating as a meditator proved to be quite the experience since my increased breadth of awareness allowed me to clearly see all these patterns that came up. And as with when dealing with difficult experiences, the best way to relate to all of it was not to push it away or criticise myself even further, but just for me to recognise those patterns of mind for what they were. And to do it with humour.

Shortly after my enjoyable but ultimately unsuccessful internet dating career, a friend of mine introduced me to someone called Lucy who I ended up marrying a few years later. I had learnt a lot through my dating experience and as our relationship developed I thought I was now in great shape to be a kind, compassionate partner. *I've got this down.* More hubris.

The first thing I saw was that I was not quite as saintly as I initially thought. I had told myself a very convincing story of how calm and collected I was but that was effectively because I was living in a bubble where I just did what I wanted when I wanted. Now that I was in a proper relationship where I had to take another person into account, I soon realised that there were still lots of things which frustrated the hell out of me. Whether it's our romantic partner or just someone on the bus, other people really know how to push our buttons. While we can be fairly effective at winding ourselves up, it is other people that are the true masters. Relationships with others are therefore perhaps the best places for seeing ourselves.

The mobile mindfulness approach as shared in this book absolutely includes bringing greater awareness to how we relate to others. While formal sitting practice definitely does help us in our relationships, it is the mobile real-time practice that can really accelerate what we discover. I learnt this the hard way.

Too many times when in conversation with Lucy or over dinner I would be distracted and my mind would be elsewhere. I had become really skilled in being present with myself but no good at being present with another person. Her frustration with my frankly poor behaviour meant I really had to up my mindfulness game. I put a lot of energy into it and soon it became as important as any other part of my practice. What I decided to do was bring as much attention as I could to the times when I was with her. And when I noticed distractions and boredom surfacing, I would just let them come and go as I would with anything else. When we allow other people into our mindfulness practice like this, we start to realise that everything we have learnt by connecting with ourselves can also be in service of us connecting with others. Not only is it a beautiful thing, we are also much less likely to get told off for being an idiot. But we don't have to wait until we are told, nor indeed does this have to happen in the context of romantic relationships. It is not always possible to see all our patterns ourselves and so this is where buying some coffee and cake for our trusted friends is more than worth the investment.

———

Internet dating is just one example of how apps and social networks have a bad reputation when it comes to genuine connection. If we were to read the comments below a news article or do a Twitter search on a contentious celebrity, it wouldn't take too long before we started to despair for the world. These spaces unfortunately can tend to abound with vitriol and negative feeling and while I've not yet done a detailed survey I'm sure that for every adorable cat picture online, there are likely to be at least two vile diatribes against often well-intentioned people. There is a good argument that the ease of posting one's opinion and the relative anonymity that comes with many messaging platforms have led to much of the online world being a place that is more divisive than uniting. But the vast amount of online content and digital tools available today means that we will always find either heaven or hell, dependent on what we want to look for. We made the web and then filled it with ourselves. Therefore it should be no surprise that it contains the beautiful as well as the not-so beautiful. Just as it is easy to look at ourselves and only see the flaws, when it comes to the web we tend to focus on the trolls and the haters. But Kirsten's blog that I mentioned in the previous chapter has already shown us that there is hope in social networks. The stories she shares of her life with chronic pain help support thousands of other young people with similar conditions around the world and her blog is motivated by a genuine compassion for others. If our brains contain the full range from animal to angel, then so too does the interweb.

We all have an opportunity to turn things around. We can safely assume that there will always be negativity in our digital world. We all have the capacity for the not-so-great and now that so many of us have ways to give a voice to our opinions, some of that will be a little ugly. But we also know that the web can be a means for real connection when we let it. I don't find it particularly useful to argue about whether a Facebook friend is the same as a friend sourced through non-digital means. But I do find it useful to reflect on what might be possible now we live in a world where there are not only seven billion people but also where soon enough the majority of those people will have access to mobile devices. What new opportunities for connection might the next years hold? As a popular technology, the web is hardly in its adolescence and I am confident that it will mature in time.

———

When relaxation, focus, presence and the ability to deal with the difficult become well established we can sometimes need a little nudge to move our awareness outside of ourselves. This is the purpose of the main technique for this chapter.

Wishing everybody well
Core technique #5: Kindness practice

As with the six-sense noting practice, this core technique actively uses thinking as a device to develop the positive qualities that we are aiming for. The main difference is that it involves us using our imagination a little bit, whereas all the other techniques are about knowing what is directly happening in our experience with nothing else added on. For that reason some people find it entirely natural and absolutely adore it while others find it a bit more tricky to get the hang of. I was definitely one of those who did find it tricky but over time I have grown to love it in my own way.

Now that we're switching from just reading to both reading and meditating, take a short while to make sure you're here. Feeling the body, the book in the hands, the feet on the ground, the bum on the seat.

Feel the breath, however it is, and receive whatever sounds are around.

Notice if your mind is particularly calm or whether it's more active. Neither is better than the other – what's important is the knowing.

Take even more time to settle down. Notice how present you are right now and enjoy any quiet pleasure that brings.

This technique is made up of four different phases. What we do in each phase is choose a person to focus on and deliberately send them our kind thoughts. Then we notice what happens. That's it.

We'll start with someone we find easy to feel kindness towards. It could be a family member, a friend, a romantic partner or anyone else you wish the absolute best for. They can be dead or alive, near or far, it doesn't really matter. What does matter is that they are important to you and just thinking of them makes the world a better place. There's no right answer but a good clue is that the first person you thought of is probably a good choice.

Now that you have the first person to whom you'll send your kindness, bring that person to mind. Do whatever feels right for you, whether that's imagining them in front of you, remembering a time with them that was particularly meaningful or by any other means.

Now that you have them in mind, you will wish them well by repeating some simple phrases in their direction. The most classic phrases that are used are *may you be well* and *may you be happy.*

So let's give them a go. Direct these thoughts of kindness to the person who means so much to you.

May you be well.

May you be happy.

Repeat the phrases every few seconds or so, keeping the body relaxed and open and just offering those phrases out to the recipient of your kindness.

May you be well.

May you be happy.

The words are not meant to have any kind of magical power, somehow transmitting their loveliness through the ether. What they do is incline our minds towards kindness, and get us used to having an open, generous and compassionate mind. So starting with the person for whom that comes most naturally is the best way to get going.

May you be well.

May you be happy.

If the phrases feel a bit clunky, mix them up a bit and use words that mean more to you. Other variants I like are: *may you know peace* and *may all be good where you are.*

Or you can make them more specific while avoiding getting too stuck in the story. What matters is that the kind sentiment comes easily and whatever words help you do that the best are the best ones to use. Short and memorable is also a good way to go.

You may find the words clunky whatever they are. This was my initial experience. I found it all a bit artificial and not what I understood mindfulness to be all about. I've since learnt that this is an entirely normal reaction and the best thing to do is just to give it a go and to include that resistance as another thing to know and learn about ourselves.

May you be well.

May you be happy.

Repeat the phrases as often as feels comfortable or necessary.

May you be well.

May you be happy.

Now notice what else is happening. How the body is. How the mind is. Whether there is a feeling of warmth or openness and if there is, take the time to enjoy what that is like.

If there's nothing much happening, then notice that too. You now know that it's not about what we know but that we know it in the first place.

May you be well.

May you be happy.

Take your time. No need to rush through the exercise.

May you be well.

May you be happy.

Now take a little break as we switch up into the second phase. In this phase the object of your kind thoughts will be you.

Notice what it feels like to hear that. If there is any resistance to that idea, just acknowledge that.

And simply offer the same words which you offered to another now to yourself.

May I be well.

May I be happy.

You may notice that you have an inclination to rush through this part because it feels awkward to turn that well-wishing towards yourself. If that happens, just acknowledge that and slow it down. Taking as much time to say the phrases as feels OK.

May I be well.

May I be happy.

Use whatever variant feels best.

May I be well.

May I be happy.

Notice what else is happening.

It's very interesting to know that when this practice is most classically taught, the first phase is wishing yourself well and only afterwards do you open out to the loved one. However, the reason I've presented it the other way around here is that so many of us find it difficult to be kind to ourselves and so starting there would be the trickier way in. As explored in the previous chapter, all too often we consider ourselves unworthy of the good things in life and therefore might feel guilty when turning kindness inwards. The intention here is not of self-indulgence but of self-care.

There are many dimensions to how we can benefit from this 'loving-kindness' technique. The first is that we simply incline the mind towards kindness. The second is that we can develop some nice concentration by the use of the repeated phrases and resting the mind in any positive feelings that result. The third dimension of the loving-kindness technique is what we can learn about our reaction to the instruction. So if you notice that any feelings of unworthiness or doubt or this-is-a-useless-exercise come up, then recognise them and let them be as they are. That is so much more important than simply being able to repeat phrases.

May I be well.

May I be happy.

Take your time through the exercise.

May I be well.

May I be happy.

The third phase of this exercise is to open out our kindness, making the object of it someone we don't have any particular love for or beef with. This can be done in a number of ways. A classic way is to imagine all the people located in various directions from you when repeating the phrases.

May all the people in front of me be happy.

May all those behind me be well.

May all the people to the left of me know peace.

May all those to the right know love.

That is definitely a nice way to do it but my preference is to do something a little bit different. So let's bring to mind everyone who made it possible for this book to come into your hands.

You may have bought the book from a shop or borrowed it from the library so bring to mind the people who served you there.

May you be well.

May you be happy.

You may have bought this book online so think about the hundreds of people who made the website you used possible.

May you all be well.

May you all be happy.

Bring to mind the people who work in the distribution centres, the people who drove the vehicles which moved this book along with its friends from the printers to the warehouses and then to the stores.

May you all be well.

May you all be happy.

Think about everyone at the publishing company who worked on the book. The designers, the marketers, the editors, the editorial assistants.

May you all be well.

May you all be happy.

Think of all the people who made the paper which you are holding. A countless list of workers.

May you all be well.

May you all be happy.

Now bring to mind all the people who have read this book. If it helps, you can imagine them all reading along at the same time as you. All sharing this intention to look after themselves and look after others. A beautiful thing.

May we all be well.

May we all be happy.

It is unlikely that you'll ever meet any of these people and even if they walked past you in the street you would have no idea.

Wish them well using the phrases which mean the most to you and notice how you feel.

We'll now move on to the fourth and final phase of this technique. And of course we've saved the best for last.

The object of this phase is someone you have a difficult relationship with. Yes. That person.

Bring them to mind and no matter how hard it might feel, try wishing them well.

May you be well.

May you be happy.

And notice whatever resistance you can right now.

May you be well.

May you be happy.

Just be gentle with yourself and the person you have trouble with. Use this meditation as a safe way to see if that relationship can be different in any way. It may well be true that they have been wrong to you in the past. This meditation is not intended to excuse them for what they have done. It is not intended that we act as a doormat and just take whatever is dealt our way lying down. This meditation is all about training us in kindness and knowing what the boundaries of that are for us right now.

May you be well.

May you be happy.

Feel what the body is like.

Feel how the mind is right now, whether it feels open or if it feels contracted.

May you be well.

May you be happy.

———

Some people do find this loving-kindness technique challenging at first. I did so myself. After learning mindfulness with all its emphasis on the direct knowing of things just as they are, I found the idea of generating and directing these thoughts a bit too artificial for my tastes. However, I stuck with it and while it has not yet become a primary formal practice for me, I do use it relatively regularly, especially when out and about.

As I mentioned before, as a maker of apps which are used all around the world, I rarely get the chance to meet the vast majority of people who enjoy them. Chris O'Sullivan is, however, an exception. Chris is based in Edinburgh and often works from Glasgow where I live and we met through a mutual contact.

He began using a mindfulness app which he got into relatively quickly, particularly enjoying the exercises designed for walking and other aspects of regular city life. Thanks to his discovery of mindfulness, he'd found a way to use what he had previously considered as dead time to be in the moment rather than just get sucked into social media and all the rest.

Chris has always been generous and empathetic but he was struggling with the loving-kindness practice. He felt connected to people when there was a natural inclination towards that but wishing strangers well seemed contrived. He knew that he was missing something but he wasn't quite sure what it was. He then got a major jolt which changed everything.

It was 22 December 2014 and we were leaving the office in Glasgow for the Christmas party. As we were waiting in the office foyer a tragedy unfolded, right outside the door. At its heart a human tragedy, but also an international news story and a major incident. A large refuse collection lorry went out of control in the heart of the city, mounting the pavement and hitting pedestrians Christmas shopping, before crashing into a hotel. It was truly awful. Having spent time as a first aid volunteer, I knew I was likely to be able to do something to help. So I went in. For around ten minutes, a group of us were in that junction rendering emergency first aid to some of those who were severely injured until official responders arrived.

Those minutes went by as if in slow motion, but somehow my consciousness expanded exponentially. I could see options, actions, people and consequences laid out like a carpet. I could see death, life, compassion, and a city rising in shock and solidarity, and I could see it all at once. Most of the usually hidden aspects of humanity were there. All in the space of a few moments.

For that day I lived moment to moment. I genuinely believe that the mindfulness practice I had started allowed me to recognise and accept how I was feeling, helped me contextualise and manage that trauma. In the days that followed I used the techniques to allow and accept feelings as they came.

Weeks later I realised that I could now see the part of mindfulness I had been missing up to that point – the power of the moment, the sheer volume of what it can contain, and the sense of connection with others and the world it can create. If we had been just a few metres over, or left a minute earlier, we might have been hit. But we weren't. I felt able to see that and accept it.

I realised that the surge of humanity I'd seen reaching out to those hurt, confused or dying was what all this loving-kindness stuff was about. Being connected, being part of a world. I remember feeling compassion not just for those injured by the crash, but also for those who stepped up, professionally trained or not. Members of the public turned their backs to block the view from others. People came forward to escort distressed but uninjured people to safety. Two young first aid volunteers waded into a major incident their training never prepared them for.

When I saw myself on the front pages of the papers rendering emergency first aid I saw that moment again, but from another viewpoint.

There was a sense of connection around the city as a whole. It appears in times of tragedy such as this and also in times of celebration.

When the name of the person I tried to help was released I thought it would undo me. It was definitely uncomfortable but I was able to take it in. I felt able to wish their family well, to feel empathy, but not to flounder. Then the next time I tried a kindness meditation which involved setting aside the personal narrative and focusing on altruistically wishing strangers well, I found it worked. I realised how self-absorbed I'd been and how jolted I'd been by what happened on that day in Glasgow.

Thankfully not all of us have to go through the terrible experience that Chris had to see the value of connection with others. But it does raise an interesting question. What *does* it take for us to see a stranger as a someone rather than a no one?

———

Ten Meditations
Designed to shorten the gap between ourselves and everyone else

Shoot Kindness

There is a genre of computer games called 'first-person shooter'. Even if you're not a gamer, you know the kind of thing I'm talking about. You typically play some kind of military character and go around shooting people, with the first person bit meaning that what you see on the screen is meant to be what the character sees through their eyes. This is a walking meditation technique which is a little bit like that but we just replace the bullets with kind thoughts. What I love about it is that everyone around us helps us give our compassion a little workout. As you walk along as part of your normal day, just pick someone you can see at random and send them a kind silent thought such as, *Have a great day*, *I hope you get what you want* or simply *Be well*. Short, snappy, simple. Then just do the same thing for other people that you notice along your walk, finding a rhythm that feels natural and not too overwhelming. You needn't worry if it feels a bit artificial at first, just stick with it. So just like in the game, you zap everyone that you can, but this time what you're zapping people with is the power of your kindness. When walking around town we can often get caught up in our personal soap opera and this really helps us get out of that, even for a little bit. Oh, and it's also really great fun.

🏠 Arriving Well

Transitions are important. Each time we move from one place to another is an opportunity to reset ourselves. One of the most important transitions is the one between finishing work and coming home. We often talk about getting out 'on the wrong side of the bed' and how that can affect how we get on for the rest of the day but we very rarely talk about what I call 'The Arrive'. I cannot underestimate the importance of The Arrive. When we've had a really tough day at work, we build up all sorts of tension and other negative feeling. What we typically do is bring all that into our home when we come through the door and it then colours the whole of our evening. If we live by ourselves, all the momentum of the day and its challenges mean we continue to feel uncomfortable and will probably sleep poorly. If we live with others, because we're carrying all that negativity we risk lashing out at the people we love and ruining the evening. We've all been there. This is what makes the ten or fifteen minutes when we come through the door so critical. Or if you've got a busy house the moment you arrive, then it is the period when you are walking or travelling home that is vital. If you have a busy work life, then I'd go as far as to say that this time is the most important few minutes of the day. Our work already takes so much from us so let's do something about it. Take a few minutes to just sit and settle down. Listen to your body. Listen to the sounds around you. Watch the momentum of the day express itself through all manner of thoughts. Watch your hand twitch to check your phone to see if any more emails related to the project you're working on have come through. Just watch that happen without feeling the need to actually follow through. Set an intention for what you want from your evening. Then when you meet your partner or your flatmate or your child for the first time, notice the impulse to tell them about that annoying thing that happened to you and don't. Compared to great acts of charity, this may appear all very innocuous. But don't be fooled by appearances. Arriving well is one of the most generous things you will ever do. To yourself and to others.

 Yay FM

There is a term in the mindfulness tradition called 'sympathetic joy'. I've always found it to be an unfortunately clunky way of describing a beautiful thing – seeing and celebrating the fact that other people are having a great time. I call it 'Yay FM' since it's not always super obvious and so we have to tune into it like back in the day when you still had to do that with radio stations. The first part of this technique is to notice when other people are happy. This can be as simple as noticing a stranger smiling when walking down the street or something more obvious like our best friend getting their dream job. When we notice these things the practice is to try and resonate with their good feeling and let it affect us. This is relatively easy when someone close to us has good news or when we enjoy the contagiousness of people we come across in our day who are laughing and smiling. It gets difficult, however, when other people are happy but we find it hard to join them. When our Facebook feed becomes full of baby photos and here we are single and alone or struggling to conceive ourselves. When the other guy gets the promotion that you were desperate for. This is where the real practice is. And remember, it's not about being joyful for everyone in every circumstance. The real insight lives in when we notice where our boundaries are and see if we can move them slowly out over time.

 Grateful Sleep

This is another one of those practices that sounds a bit soppy but when done consistently can change our lives. While best done just before going to bed, it works well as a formal practice. What we do is bring to mind someone who we are grateful to. It could be a friend, mentor, family member, whoever. The important thing is for it to feel easy and natural to thank them. It could even be someone famous that you've never personally met, but that tends to only work well if you have a strong personal connection to their work. Bring that person to mind and reflect on what they have done to help you. And just say thank you. Just keeping the person, the object of your gratitude, in mind and saying thank you, either out loud or just silently to yourself. Do this for as long as feels OK and every now and then notice how you feel. If there is warmth or calm or a general feeling of loveliness, notice that and let yourself really enjoy that. You can stay with one person or, if you like, move on to another. If you are doing this technique just before bed, it can be nice to run through people who have been helpful to you throughout the day. Ending the day on a positive note like this can be conducive to good sleep since the mind feels comfortable, warm and relaxed, qualities which are close to sleep itself.

Hidden Ingredients

Pick up any packet of food and you will find all sorts of information about what's inside. But very rarely will your ingredients list include the people who have made it possible. You can do this practice either while eating, cooking or simply holding some food. Actively imagine all the people who have made it possible for your food to get to you. Start with the farmers or pickers who could be from half a world away. Reflect on their effort and dedication at the start of the food process, working with nature and often in difficult conditions. Reflect on their motivations, how they work for the wellbeing of their families and the community around them. Then move up the chain to the people who helped pack and process the food and do the same. Next are the transportation heroes, the women and men who move the food all the

way to the store where you buy it. Then finally reflect
on the people who helped sell you the food, stacking
shelves, working long repetitive hours on the till. The
man who pushes the supermarket trolleys around. Then
finally the cook, even if that is you. When framed in this
way, food can be a wonderful way to bring into awareness
how connected we are with so many people that we may
never meet in person. And it makes even the most humble of meals taste so much better.

Love Email

Few things fill us with as much dread as the humble
inbox. Email is possibly the best and worst designed
communication system of all time. It is good in the
sense that its mechanic is quite simple and it is evil since
for so many millions of people around the world, the
knowledge that it exists and that those pesky messages
are constantly piling up drains their attention, energy
and sometimes their will to live. Let us not even speak
of the reply-to-all. This practice is most useful when you
are having difficulty with email, most typically with those
related to work. Before reading a message from someone
you know and are finding challenging, take a short few
seconds to think about them as a person. A human being
sending a message to try and get the job done, even if
they are doing it in the most excruciating way. You can
do the same when sending. Before pressing send, reflect
on the intention with which you've written the message
and in as much as you can, send it with kindness to the

recipient. Our inboxes can be brutal places so why not bring some lightness to them whenever possible, even if that feels forced at times.

The Internet of Humans

We've all had our personal struggles with social media. Sometimes I make the mistake of reading the comments on a news article or do a Twitter search on a contentious issue. Suddenly I'm pulled down into the depths of the online world with all its negativity and venom and I deal with it by meeting it with a cold shoulder. The opposite is also true. There will often be the most lovely of news floating down my Facebook news feed and instead of rejoicing in the good fortune of my friends my eyes will just scan down mechanically, immune to the positive sentiment that is clearly there. Having reflected on how I engage with social media and communications in general, I now make the distinction between the internet of information and the internet of people. It can be so easy to just read information as information, forgetting that behind each post, tweet, image or story is a human being looking to express themselves. It is absolutely the case that not all those human beings are aligned to our view of the world but I have certainly found that seeing my social feeds and my inbox as a group of people instead of a blah of information makes it a much more connected experience, if not always a more comfortable one. See what you can do to spot the human in all the information. Whether it's the author of a clickbait article just trying to get by, a celebrity posting another selfie to feel like they are recognised, or a friend sharing a photo of their breakfast because they are a little bit lonely and want some interaction, see what you can do to sense the human among all the information.

Real Listening

This is perhaps the most important way in which my mindfulness practice has impacted my relationships. It is perhaps a cliché that good communication is the secret to a successful and loving relationship but that doesn't make it any less true. Early on in my adventures in mindfulness it became really quite stark how bad I was at listening. While it looked like I was in a conversation, all I was actually doing was waiting for the other person to stop talking so I could say the important thing that I had to say. It was less a conversation and more a monologue which another person just happened to have the good fortune to be near. The secret to skilful listening is balancing three types of hearing. The first is hearing the words the other person is saying. The second is being aware of how they are saying them, most importantly how their body is. Is it closed or open? Does anything look tight or do they look relaxed? The final component to listening is listening to ourselves, noticing how the mind reacts and wants to get involved. Being present with another human being as they are speaking is one of the most generous things we can do for another and learning how to do it well has been a real education for me, helping me become more intimate not only with other people but also with myself.

 Thank Yourself

Sitting meditation tends to be best when done with others. Even if you're not interacting with each other during the formal session, there is something special about being in a space with other people who share the same intention towards awareness and connection. Saying that, however, this technique is more concerned with ourselves. When it comes to saying thank you, it's a relatively easy thing to say to other people, but what about ourselves? Once your mind has settled down a little bit, take ten or so minutes recalling times when you have been helpful to others. It can be big moments in your life such as that time you lent your friend the money they needed to save their business. Or it can be the little things such as a smile of acknowledgement to the person who sold you your coffee in the morning. You can even say thank you to something you did for yourself such as that really quite tough workout you sweated through yesterday to support your health for the future. Just recall these different incidents, say thank you to yourself and notice what happens. If you're doing this as a mobile practice, you simply thank yourself every time you notice that you've done something generous and kind. Be ready to be surprised how often during the day this actually happens. Whether done as a formal or mobile practice, it is quite likely that you will also come upon some internal resistance. This will look like thoughts which say that you don't deserve this thanks and that you're being needless-ly self-indulgent. When these do come up, notice them and be kind to them as well.

 Face Off

This is the first two-player meditation which I've included in this book. There are already lots of techniques here which see us involving other people in our mindfulness but they mainly do so without actually knowing that's what they are doing! Two-player meditations are differ-ent in that both people are doing the same instruction together and, critically, it only works if the other person is there. This is an extension of a technique introduced earlier in the book and is best done in a fairly formal way, by which I mean in a relatively quiet place where you are both comfortable and are unlikely to be disturbed. Sit opposite each other, close enough to see each other's faces but far enough to see their whole body. Start by both of you closing your eyes, then decide who is Player 1 and who is Player 2. Player 1 opens their eyes and looks at Player 2 with the intention to just see them as they are. Notice any tendency to create and follow a story about the other person and just let that go. See if you can see them just as they are. Player 1 does that for a minute or two and then closes their eyes, telling Player 2 when they have finished. Then Player 2 does the same. The third part of the technique is that when Player 2 has finished, they invite Player 1 to open their eyes as well so that both of you have your eyes open. Then spend a further minute just looking at each other, seeing if you are able to view the other person without labels, and when those labels come up, just letting them go and going back to the act of simple seeing. This can be a very intimate practice and can be quite full-on so only do as much as feels right. There are fewer more powerful acts than looking into the eyes of another and knowing that you are accepted for whatever you are. When you do this practice you might notice that it takes a while to feel comfortable and not super awkward. It's OK to laugh if that is what feels like the right thing to do to deal with it. As long as you notice that.

Chapter 7

This is Going Deeper

While I do consider myself a morning person, waking up at three o'clock is still a little bit of a stretch. But when you're staying as a guest at a monastery deep in the forests of north-east Thailand that is just what you have to do. It is a fairly hardcore place. The early morning bell is just the start of it. There is only one meal a day, taken at seven in the morning and dependent on whatever food is given by the visiting public. Otherwise the daily schedule is fairly open but the expectation is that you will fill your day with meditation, doing long hours of formal practice in and around the little hut set into the forest that you are allocated. Once a week residents are encouraged to take part in a group meditation session that runs all through the night and twice a week there is a cup of tea available in the afternoon. Oh, and if you want to stay longer than three days, as a means to demonstrate commitment, you have to shave your head. That means everything from your neck upwards. Which of course includes eyebrows. Staying here is not for the half-hearted.

The twice-weekly afternoon tea is a fairly basic affair. But it is a great opportunity to spend time with the resident monks and other guests, outside of the formalities of the more ritual elements that are typical of any monastic environment such as this. This particular monastery is unusual in that it is set up especially for the training of Western-born monks in the Thai forest tradition. This means that I found myself sharing my simple mug of black tea with monks originally from across all parts of Europe and North America. The tea was of course black since milk is considered a food and is not allowed after the day's single meal. Perhaps only half the community came to the tea and the more senior monks kept themselves to themselves, leaving us short-term guests to mingle with each other as well as the two novice monks who were due to take their full ordination later in the year.

I started talking to one of the novices and we discovered a remarkable coincidence. Just like mine, his parents moved from Sri Lanka to the UK in the late sixties. Just like me, he was born in 1980. It then got super weird when we discovered that we grew up in the same suburban town just outside London not two miles away from each other. My parents had two choices of school to put me through and he went to the one that I ended up not going to. It's crazy. He was effectively the same person as me other than the rather big difference that he was a monk.

We ended up having an argument. It was all very polite and well mannered given the circumstances but it was an argument all the same. It boiled down to this: I believe that it's possible to fully walk the contemplative path whilst living a regular life and he doesn't. He feels that the only way to wholeheartedly practise in the insight meditation tradition is through the monastic route. He considers anything else a cop-out. This novice monk and I, each the mirror of each other, spent a good hour arguing our cases and while we each understood and respected where the other was coming from, our positions did not change. His is not an untypical view. Forest monks are professional followers of the Buddhist path and so their whole lifestyle is set up in such a way as to realise the fruits of that path. On the other hand, as a so-called householder I could only at best be a keen amateur, given that my progress would inevitably be inhibited by the trappings and responsibilities of modern life. I disagree. I believe that while the monastic path is a beautiful thing and a tradition that should be preserved, it does not hold a monopoly on the deep spiritual results of practice. The teachings that make up the Buddhist traditions are ultimately about what it is to be a human being and the wisdom and insights that are available through meditation and other styles of contemplative practice are not dependent on any particular environment or condition. Or in other words, it's possible to get the deeper results of practice while living in the busiest of cities. I believed that then and I believe it even more today.

Back in 2007, I was working for a large technology consultancy and, given the intensity of the work, it was fairly common for people to take some time off from the company for up to a year to do something completely different before coming back to resume their career. It was the same company that I had joined straight after university and while I was still enjoying my time there, I decided to take advantage of their leave of absence policy. My interest in meditation had really been growing over that time and I decided to spend six months training in a variety of monasteries and meditation centres in Sri Lanka, Thailand and Burma. I knew that the urban meditation style that I'd been pursuing was the way for me, but also knew that I still had a lot to learn and so wanted to take a trip while I was still young and relatively responsibility-free. I ended up spending three to four weeks in each centre I visited. While they all operated within the insight meditation tradition, each had their own particular style and angle and the biggest thing I took away from my whole experience was a simple understanding of that. When you look at a wide and diverse set of mindfulness approaches and techniques on paper, it can seem that because they are so different from each other they have nothing in common with each other. In some cases, the underlying principles behind the practices even seem to be in opposition to each other. However, over that six months of dedicated practice I started to see how all the different teachings and approaches fitted together. It really did at times feel like puzzle parts clicking satisfyingly together.

I did have some doubts, though. My meeting with my monastic doppelgänger had set some alarm bells racing. *What if he's right? What if I just want to have it all and making progress on the spiritual path isn't possible alongside the inbox, the love life and the mortgage? What if I'm just deluding myself?* Thankfully the next stop on my monastery crawl dissolved that doubt. This time I was staying at a fully Thai monastery in the far south of the country which was headed up by a highly respected abbot. It may not surprise you to hear that I am a bit of a geek when it comes to meditation. Thanks to my geekery I have a few different meditation lineages which are my absolute favourites and not only was this monastery part of one of them, the abbot had a wonderful reputation within it. I was therefore very excited when I was granted an audience with him. I was also very nervous. During our conversation I explained the style of meditation that I was doing and the progress I was making. His teaching style was very different to what I was personally doing as it emphasised the development of super-deep concentration states and the subsequent use of states as the jump-off point for wisdom and insight. I had never done anything remotely like it. I felt intimidated. I was nervous that he would consider my own meditation approach as being second rate. That actually couldn't have been further from the truth and what he ended up telling me was this: *I live in the forest so I teach a way that works in the forest. You live in the city and so you are practising in a way that works well for the city. Don't try and practise as if you lived in the forest when you don't. The forest style and the city style are both good. They take different routes but they both lead to where you want to go. Keep it up and good luck.*

———

Let's talk about going deep.

There was a time when mindfulness was only available as part of a religious package but now that package has become unbundled, it can be found in a range of new spaces and contexts. Mindfulness is finding its feet in the office, on the sports field and in our everyday life, places which are nowhere near the monastery or shrine room. But while mindfulness has become much more than just a spiritual practice, it still can be a spiritual practice if we want it to be. This is because the modern mindfulness movement as we know it today has its origins in what is known as insight meditation, which is rooted in the Buddhist tradition. To ignore that would be both a shame and an omission and therefore this chapter will explore insight meditation and where it can lead.

If you don't think the more spiritual aspects of meditation practice are of interest to you, then you are of course free to skip this chapter. I would, however, argue that everyone keen to make mindfulness part of their lives should at least understand a little bit about its spiritual dimensions. Even if you don't plan to actively pursue them, what they point to will ultimately help you understand mindfulness that bit better. I believe any book that tries to help people use mindfulness to improve their lives but doesn't include the deeper elements is incomplete. Our wish to look deeper into the mysteries of life is just as valid a reason to meditate as wanting to be less stressed and less distracted.

At the start of this book I talked about how there are two reasons people get into mindfulness: curiosity and

Our wish to look deeper into the mysteries of life is just as valid a reason to meditate as wanting to be less stressed and less distracted.

crisis. Most people come in through the crisis door and when mindfulness helps them soften their problem, they may just leave it at that. But just as likely is that once people get the results that they were looking for, their interest is piqued as to where else mindfulness may lead. Because if we want to go there, all the different mindfulness practices we've explored so far can lead to us looking deeper and therefore to gaining insight. Relaxing the mind gives us the quietness we need as a foundation. Focus gives us the mental stamina to look at things for a decent amount of time. Presence is where life happens and so is essential to any contemplative practice. The ability to cope with difficult experience shows us that we can have balance in even the most turbulent times. The practices of connection start to break down the boundaries between ourselves and everything and everyone around us. So while we may have entered through the door marked 'crisis', what we experience may conjure up new questions and the time may come when we start knocking on the door marked 'curiosity'.

Curiosity is where it began for me. From a young age I'd always been interested in how things work. *Why are people unhappy even though they have all the things that they thought would make them happy? Why did I feel so sad when England got knocked out of yet another football tournament? What turns off when I go to sleep and comes back when I wake up?* I had studied science at university as well as a little bit of philosophy, but for me it wasn't until I discovered meditation and its emphasis on the naked unmediated experience of my mind and its contents that I got really excited. Finally I'd found a way to explore these questions through direct observation and inquiry instead of through the medium of argument and counterargument. I was hooked.

If we make the effort to bring mindfulness to all parts of our life and work on all the skills as outlined in the previous chapters, then we can get to a pretty great place. We will be relaxed. We will have a decent amount of focus when we need it. We will be present in life as it happens and be able to cope with the tougher things that come our way. We will feel a genuine connection with others. This is a lovely place to be and through mindfulness we become the kind of person that it is both good to be and good to be around.

There is, however, if you want to go there, an entirely different game available. Game A is the one we've been playing so far and it is a game all about becoming a more sensitive, relaxed and balanced person. Game B, however, is about exploring what it is to be a person in the first place, about exploring identity itself. We've already had glimpses of this along the way. When coping with the difficult we've seen how much freedom comes from observing thoughts and emotions rather than getting caught up in them. By taking the position of the observer we can then realise that *I am not my thoughts*, and that realisation can bring an enormous sense of relief and the problem stops being as overwhelming as it previously was. This is when we begin to see that if we stop identifying so closely with something, we have less of a hard time. Game B pulls on that thread. If we are not our thoughts and emotions, then what are we? What else can be let go of? What happens when we stop identifying so tightly with other aspects of our experience? Is the present moment all there is?

A couple of chapters ago I talked about how the secret to mindfulness was that life gets better when we start taking it less personally. While this might sound like a flippant remark it really does summarise meditation, including the deeper elements. The hypothesis at the heart of the mindfulness tradition is that the amount of suffering we experience is directly proportional to how much we identify with things and consider them to be ours. So if you get a fancy new car and make it a big part of defining who you are, then if it gets even a tiny little scratch you're going to feel some serious pain. But if you still have the car but see it just as a car rather than as part of you and your story, then that scratch will be a bit annoying but ultimately not a massive deal.

The idea of practice is to take this hypothesis and see how true it is. Over time we get more and more information and plot the graph with suffering on one axis and the prominence of our sense of self on the other. What we start to find is that the time when we feel most suffering is when things are all about Me and when we feel most joy and peace is when that Me is much quieter. That then raises the central question of mindfulness as a spiritual practice: if suffering is linked to how strong our level of identification with things is, what happens if there is no identification at all?

This is the rabbit hole that Game B invites us to go down. What we find are the insights which gave insight meditation its name. This is, however, not for the faint-hearted. Using mindfulness to solve our problems and using it to investigate the core programming of what makes up our experience are not the same thing. Relaxing our identification with things or letting go is a beautiful thing to do. But as we go deeper and deeper into meditation practice, just as in any good game, the territory can get a bit challenging as the levels become more advanced. An example of one of the common challenges we may come across is what is known as spiritual materialism. This is what happens when we make progress on the spiritual path but start to sabotage it by making the idea of a successful practitioner just another part of our identity. *I am such a great meditator. Now that I'm not doing so much of that self-referential thinking, I really am the bee's knees*. When you think you've got it, that's the best clue that there is something else to let go of.

———

Wisdom is a word that is used quite regularly in the context of meditation. Wisdom is a natural result of being alive. Assuming that we have at least some ability to learn from our experience, as we get older we invariably become wiser and understand more about how life works. We learn that our friendships and relationships always come to an end, and that

By looking closely at our experience through meditation we see that everything is in a process of change and also that lasting happiness is not dependent on any external conditions.

that ending is painful. We learn that the times when we've felt most alive are the times where we've been the most present, just letting whatever happens happen. We learn that we should enjoy the good times while they are around but they do not last forever and change happens. Growing in wisdom is part of the process as we age and gather more life experience. What meditation does is supercharge that process. When we look into the processes of our mind in detail we start to see which of our actions lead to us having a bad time and which lead to us doing OK. When we really understand what leads to what, we then have no option but to act with wisdom.

The mechanic of how meditation helps us develop wisdom is actually quite straightforward. One of my all-time favourite teachers describes insight meditation as 'ways of seeing that lead to freedom'. This is a brilliant definition. Much of the trouble we get ourselves into is because we see the world in a certain way. We think things will last forever and so when they don't we get upset. We think that acquiring a new phone, partner or house will make us happy and when after a while we see that they don't we get upset. These are the classic patterns of mind that insight meditation helps us unpick. By looking closely at our experience through meditation we see that everything is in a process of change and also that lasting happiness is not dependent on any external conditions.

The growth of scientific research into the benefits and effects of meditation has been instrumental in the development of mindfulness to where it is today. Neuroscience has been at the heart of this development and detailed analysis has shown that there is no single structure within the brain which governs our sense of self and that it appears to be an emergent property. Or in other words, while it might feel like we have this thing called a 'self' or a 'me-ness', there's nothing specific that we can point to as being definitely it. Meditation helps us start to see that for ourselves. It could be argued that everything in this book to date does lead to some kind of wisdom. So what is the difference between going deeper and conventional mindfulness? When our motivations are on the deeper side of things, we still get the results of calm, concentration, composure and all the rest but wonderful as they are, they are secondary benefits. Instead what we are aiming for and orienting towards is a more profound understanding of the mechanics of happiness.

Understanding mindfulness as a way of seeing that leads to freedom is important. The insight meditation tradition is very wary of making any absolute statements about 'the ultimate nature of reality' and rightly so. To do so just creates more dogma when mindfulness is an invitation to see things for ourselves. What the tradition does say is that perhaps there is more going on than how we conventionally perceive ourselves and the world. So why not put on some different lenses and see if those lenses lead to you having a better experience or not? When we do that and start to see how different ways of looking reduce our suffering, and we do it over and over again, at some point our previous ways of seeing the world become undermined and the suffering that was tied up with them released.

Enlightenment is a word with a lot of baggage. It conjures up all sorts of images in our heads. As a culture we are so dominated by Christian ideas of heaven that enlightenment is most commonly understood as being some kind of perfect, persistent, paradise-like state. This is however not the most useful way it should be viewed. Whether wrapped in robes or in a T-shirt and jeans, mindfulness is ultimately a practical and pragmatic tradition designed to help people experience less difficulty in their lives. It works because it helps us directly look into how that difficulty comes about and through that looking we learn how to avoid it coming up in the first place. A much better word to use instead of enlightenment is 'awakening'. Enlightenment has the feeling of a massive moment in which a giant pointing finger comes out of the sky and selects you to be special, while awakening is more of a process over time. And while there definitely can be big breakthrough moments, it is a gradual process during which we dissolve the patterns of mind and self-identification which perpetuate so much of the difficulty in our lives.

The further you go in your mindfulness adventures, the more it becomes about understanding two things – identity and interdependence. In this sixth and final core technique we shall explore both.

———

Turning the camera around on itself
Core technique #6: Non-doing

As we move into the sixth and final core technique, as before we'll start by grounding our awareness in the body.

You know how to do this by now but let me remind you just in case.

The sensations of what it feels like to hold this book are happening in the present. So if we can direct our awareness towards them and know those sensations just as they are, then we too are in the present. It's as simple as that.

Feel the texture of the book in our hands.

If you like, run a finger over the paper to see what that's like.

Or the sharpness of the spine.

The cover with its smoothness and its texture.

Ground yourself that little bit further by emphasising the overall sense of the body as it sits here, stands here, lies here.

For all the other core techniques so far we have used body awareness as the base level for settling ourselves down.

But here we'll take it one step further.

Our basic rest position for this technique will not be body awareness but what is known as 'balanced awareness'.

Having balanced awareness means that whatever is happening and wherever it is happening we just watch it happen.

Make the intention, just for this short reading meditation, to watch everything come up and then just make its own way out of awareness.

Watch sounds come into awareness and then leave. Know whatever happens but do not get involved.

Close your eyes just for a few moments to let sounds and hearing just happen.

Watch sensations in the body come into awareness and then leave.

Again just close your eyes to get used to taking this position of watching or observing without getting caught up with any particular sensation. Without getting caught up with any label or story associated with any particular sensation.

Now watch thoughts come up into awareness. And as with sounds, just let them come, knowing that they are there and not getting tangled in them or giving them any more charge than a random sound or physical sensation.

If you want to close your eyes to help you do that, then please do so for however long feels right.

Now with your eyes open, keeping the face and eyes relaxed, rest in the visual aspect of awareness. Whether it's the book or the space around you, just observe what can be observed. No need to get caught up in the details of the words or any particular thing you can see. Just let seeing be seeing.

That is the warm-up. What we're about to try is the most subtle of the six core techniques and is often most effective when we have a relatively stable awareness. This means that we're able to watch our inner experience with a decent amount of balance and not get too hooked into any stories about what is happening. Instead we just know what is happening.

So if you'd like to go back to the beginning of this section and try the warm-up again, that's totally fine. Sometimes when I'm doing this style of meditation as a formal practice, when my mind is all over the place I might do as much as twenty minutes of warm-up before moving on to this main phase.

This technique is called 'non-doing'.

It is more common that 'being' is thought of as the opposite of 'doing'. *Hey, man, stop doing and just be.* However, as our mindfulness develops and we start to see more and more subtle aspects of our mind and our experience, even the intention to 'just be' can be seen as quite a clunky form of doing. That is why I prefer the distinction of doing and non-doing. And if this paragraph doesn't make any sense right now, that's totally fine. It will do as you become more interested in this stuff over time.

So let's do it. Or not do it. Either way, this is the technique: be aware but don't do anything.

Be aware but don't do anything.

Rest in the simplicity of awareness.

Rest in the simplicity of knowing this experience.

Without doing anything.

The vast majority of mindfulness techniques are all about doing things. Put your attention on your breath and when it drifts away bring it back. Notice what kind of thought patterns come up on a regular basis and make friends with them. Feel the sensations of your feet on the ground. Send kind thoughts to this particular person. Sense the part of your body where there is most tension and actively relax that area. Mindfulness is full of this kind of stuff. So is this book.

All of these techniques are valuable to do and while it is not a criticism of them, what they do share is that they are directional. They tell us what to do. In doing so they make one aspect of experience more special than another. If you're doing a breath-based meditation, then the breath is more special than the sensations in your elbow, for example. When we are listening to sounds as we did in the warm-up just now, hearing is more special than smelling or tasting or thinking.

But what if we didn't make anything more special than anything else? That is the basis of this technique. Just resting the mind here as it is and watching whatever happens with brightness and interest.

Our awareness bright and alert. Letting everything happen. Non-doing.

Watching everything as if it was the most important thing in the universe.

Eyes open or eyes closed, it makes no difference.

Every now and then we will notice our mind switch into doing. We'll know this because something will become special. Our awareness will go out to a particular sound and start labelling it. Or it will notice a physical sensation and move that into the foreground. Or a thought such as, *What am I supposed to be doing again?* will pop up and we'll hook on to it and have a nice little discussion with ourselves about how confusing this all is.

This is doing. See if you can notice the difference between what that is like and what non-doing is like.

Try it again. Rest back into the overall sense of aware-ness and let the whole show play itself out.

This is happening. Now this is happening. No need to get involved.

When our mind is really quiet we can even start to watch the doing process in real time. What we see are little impulses or intentions, way below the level of thought, disturbing the silence of simple awareness with their outward movements.

So this is the practice: committing to non-doing and then noticing when doing happens and watching how it happens. Looking closely at how these two modes are different and how they feel different. Being brutal in your distinction and recognising that even the slightest disturbance is a doing.

Learning about doing and non-doing.

Learning about noise and silence.

Learning about that which is known and that which knows it.

While all of the techniques in this book can be used in subtle ways, this is an especially subtle practice. Its purpose is to allow our awareness itself to stand out when typically it's the various things our awareness knows that tend to be more prominent.

Given that it can sometimes be too subtle, we can also use simple questions to nudge awareness into prominence.

So when the mind is quiet and you are able to rest with awareness to the degree that you're not getting too caught up in things such as sounds and thoughts, just drop in a question.

Who is knowing?

What is this?

Questions like these are not meant to be answered in a literal way so ignore any answers that might come up. What they do is prime our curiosity and interest to start to take awareness itself as our object of attention.

Don't worry if that doesn't feel like a natural thing to do; it can take time to get the hang of it. It's much like noticing space in the room instead of the furniture within it or watching the pitch instead of the football match.

In the mindfulness tradition this is what going deeper means. Nothing is sacred when it comes to relaxing our identification with different aspects of our experience of letting go. Even the part of the mind which knows things and feels like such a fundamental part of who we are. Can we turn the camera around and become interested in who or what it is that is knowing all this stuff in the first place and how does that knowing process work? What happens when we look through the meditation lens?

———

There are many different ways into deeper practice of which the technique outlined above is just one example. Different styles of practice suit different people at different times. It is something that cannot be rushed or forced, but if you are interested there are four things which can help you make progress further and faster.

The first is regular formal practice. The mobile styles of mindfulness championed in this book are incredibly powerful but old-school sitting meditation is more effective at developing the deeper aspects of concentration. Going deep requires us to look at our experience with a fair amount of stability and most people find that is best done in the formal posture. I've never met a meditator who has gained deep insights without having done sustained formal meditation before and I doubt that's a coincidence.

The second thing that will support your deepening is working with a teacher or a tradition. The deeper insights that come from mindfulness are always best learnt from people who not only know them well themselves but have a good track record of helping other people know them too. While you might go to a yoga class in a gym for improving your flexibility, if you wanted to find out more about the spiritual aspects of the yoga tradition, the gym probably wouldn't be your first choice. In the same way, since most of the pop mindfulness movement is not targeted at the spiritual aspects of meditation, the best places to look for these are within the more religious parts of the mindfulness community. There are all sorts of different traditions and practice styles, from the secular to the very traditional, and they suit different personalities and inclinations. They also don't all necessarily finish at the same end point and so while my own background is in insight meditation, I recommend trying a few different schools and traditions to see which one feels right for you.

Next in our list of four things to help you deepen your practice is retreat. It is totally possible to gain deep insights through practice at home but since meditation retreats are environments specially designed for that very reason, they are recommended. While not everyone's lifestyle and responsibilities mean they can swan off to the forests of Asia for months at a time, just a well-guided weekend somewhere near you can make a big difference. Not only will extended periods of meditation allow you to go deeper, the unique challenges of a retreat environment can bring you right up to your edge and it is when you are at your edge that the breakthroughs tend to take place. Good teaching is also important on retreat and an indicator of whether a teacher has significant depth is whether they lead retreats.

The fourth catalyst to supercharge our going deeper is community. Much of mindfulness practice can go against the norm and so being part of a group of like-minded people can make a real difference. If you do get into mindfulness in any serious way, just as with sports like cycling or running, you will find yourself naturally wanting to connect with people who share your interest and passion. Support and be supported. These can be communities which are online, in person or a mix of the two. Out of the list of four, I would perhaps say that community is the most important since if you have that, then the other three are naturally supported.

Ten Meditations
Designed to point you to the deeper connections between things

🐾 Still Moving

There is a long history across all of the various meditation traditions of using paradox as a way to encourage our minds to look at the world a little bit differently. You'll probably be familiar with the questions 'What is the sound of one hand clapping?' and 'If a tree falls in the woods and no one is there to hear it, does it make a sound?' These particular two are now seen as a bit of a joke but when understood properly, at their heart they are questions which play with our sense of subject and object in the hope that we take on new perspectives and ways of seeing the world. This technique does the same and it is to be used when we are walking along. The conventional way of perceiving walking is that we are moving through a relatively fixed environment. In this exercise, see if you can switch that perception around by seeing the experience as your awareness being the thing that is fixed and everything else is moving through it. This can take some playing around with before you get it, but once you do it is similar to that classic optical illusion where if you look at it one way, you see a vase and if you look at it another way, you see two faces. Once you recognise those two ways of seeing you can switch between them at will and this is very similar. Watching the world move through your awareness rather than you moving though the world. It can be quite trippy for some people so please do take care and I'd suggest you don't do it when crossing the road. The same technique can be used when you are a passenger in a train or car but is absolutely not to be done when actually driving.

 Mental Hyperlinks

The word hyperlink was first coined back in the sixties. But it only hit the big time when Tim Berners-Lee included this concept of using text to link one document to another in his design for what was to become the worldwide web. Fast-forward just over twenty-five years and that simple idea of one thing being connected to another has led to a vastly sprawling network of information and ideas. All of which means that when we start off by browsing our favourite news site, one thing takes us to the next and to the next again and before we know it we're researching the nearest available litter of Shiba Inu puppies to where we live. The idea behind this technique is to notice the hyperlinks that happen in our actual thoughts. Sometimes we can catch them in real time but more often we will only be able to notice them retrospectively. For example, while writing this mindfulness technique, thinking about Tim Berners-Lee made me remember that I was once at an event where he was speaking and that led me to thinking of my friend Roland who I was working with at the time and that caused me to think about piano since Roland is a really great musician and that made me think about how bad I was at practising piano when I used to take lessons as a kid and now I'm feeling down on myself because I'm not very musical and I'm thinking that that's because I never applied myself during my classes and I wish I could play the piano today. That whole chain happened in less than five seconds. Making the intention and the time to see the hyperlink history of our minds like this can be so valuable. If I hadn't done that just now, I would be feeling bad and not quite sure why. But seeing the links between the thoughts all the way from Tim Berners-Lee to my being rubbish at music is not only fascinating and fun, it also makes my feeling bad about myself a little bit ridiculous and as a result that emotion loses some of its power over me.

Late Night Review

When going to bed, take five or so minutes to just review your day. Try and remember the different events of your day from the moment you got up to that moment when lying in bed. First notice which events stand out the most and if there is any particular emotional charge that comes with them. Avoid the temptation to engage with the story but just notice what comes up. Then notice if there are any more mundane moments of the day that you can remember. What it felt like to eat your breakfast. How your body felt when walking to work. How you felt when you walked in the door after work. This is not a memory exercise. This is an exercise in noticing connections. Taking some time to reflect on what makes a particular event stand out from the day and what makes something less memorable. Ultimately what we are trying to do is notice the relationship between how we meet experience and what that experience ends up being like. When we do this review regularly over time we then also start to see how our practice is developing and which areas of our life maybe need more care and attention.

 Watch TV

As we venture more into the deep end of mindfulness, we start to become interested in awareness itself. Just as there is a natural movement over time from self-care to care for others, there is also a natural movement from being concerned by the details of what we see to the seeing process itself. One way to encourage this change of frame is to practise it when watching TV, or indeed any screen. The default way of watching TV is to get sucked into the content. In this exercise we try to bring our mind out a little bit and notice the screen itself. The frame, the reflection, the edges. See if you can switch from watching the content to seeing the screen and back again and notice how those two modes of attention are different from each other. Once you've got the hang of that, which might take a little while, see if you can even watch the content while also being aware of the screen itself. This may seem like a funny little mindfulness game but it is surprisingly close to deep insight techniques where instead of the screen of the TV we start to pay attention to the screen of our actual awareness.

 The Me Show

Understanding the relationship between what we identify with and the pain we feel in our lives is the secret to insight practice. This technique is best done when engaging with other people, be that colleagues, friends, family or partners. The idea is just to notice whenever a strong sense of indignation comes up, or in other words when you could summarise how you are feeling by 'What about me?' Notice how that indignation feels in the body. Notice what that indignation feels like as a mindset. And notice how much awareness you have at those times and how you act when you are caught up in that indignation. Watching the play of this thing we call 'me' is a great show, often both comic and tragic in equal measure. Also, and perhaps most importantly, when we make the decision to observe it rather than just be caught up in it, it starts to lose some of its prima donna nature.

Walk Yourself

This is based on something I remember doing in pre-school. The teacher would give us an invitingly blank piece of paper and a felt-tip pen and tell us to 'take the pen for a walk'. Without taking it off the paper, we made shapes by just letting the pen go where it wanted to go without actively trying to draw anything in particular. Looking back on that now, while I'm not sure it was the teacher's intention, the exercise was pretty much a perfect meditation technique to explore the nature of self, since it really highlights the difference between the movements which just happen by themselves and those which have a bit more self-direction behind them. You might, however, consider yourself a little bit too old for doodling and so the technique suggested here is a variant of that which we can do while walking. Take yourself for a walk. It can be somewhere you need to go or, even better, just a walk for its own sake. It does, however, work best if you're in a park and so not just limited to a linear pavement or path. The purpose of the walk is two-fold. The first thing we're looking at is how so many of our movements just happen by themselves. Things like the pressing of the button at the pedestrian crossing or even the walking itself. See if you can catch any moments when you get a sense that stuff is just happening even without your active control. The more you look for it, the more you'll probably see. The second thing we're looking at is just what captures our attention on the walk. What are the things along our way that are the most 'sticky'? Get interested in why some things grab us and other things don't. There is a lot of insight to be gained when we start to see the patterns of what does and doesn't make our mind stick.

 ## Noting Together

This is another two-player meditation and builds on the core technique of six-sense noting as introduced in *This is Being Present*. Sit with another person, either in person or through digital channels. Ideally you'll be able to see their face since that helps but it's not essential. Take it in turns to say out loud a word that best represents your experience in that moment. If you're just starting out, you can use the six-sense noting words as before: *touching, seeing, hearing, smelling, tasting, thinking* and of course *confused*. If that feels a bit limiting, you can then use any words you want with the proviso that the word you say is the mental process you are noticing rather than the contents of that process. For example, if you are thinking about what you're going to make for dinner, the appropriate thing to say is *thinking* or *planning* rather than *dinner* or *fajitas*, since that is content and mindfulness is generally more interested in process rather than content. What makes it social is that you just take turns to speak your word. This is one of my all-time favourite practices and while the one-player version is still great, there are so many additional things you get from it when done together. I'll leave it to you to play around with and discover what all those benefits are but there is one thing that has always stood out for me. Not only is this a quite beautiful and intimate way of connecting to another person, whatever they say helps you prime your attention even more. What I mean by this is that if the other person notices something quite subtle like embarrassment or calm, then just by hearing that it primes my mind to be more subtle too. It's a wonderful effect. And of course, you needn't stop at two players; social noting works really well as a multiplayer meditation technique too, and having more people means that you are also able to watch how your mind is when it is listening to others and waiting for its turn.

 ## Fade Out

What happens when we fall asleep? This meditation asks this simple question and so all this technique involves is watching what happens in the falling asleep process. A good framework for doing this is through the senses. When we're in bed smell and taste have already faded somewhat and so that leaves us with the other four. When we close our eyes that fades out our vision and so there are only three senses left: hearing, feeling and thinking. The practice is therefore to let these three senses fade out as well, just as we might dial down the volume on a hi-fi when they still used to have such old-fashioned things as volume dials. Start by letting sound dial down. Letting any sounds that arise just fade out and paying attention to that fading. Once you've done that for a little while, fade out thoughts in the same way, treating them just like sounds. Noticing whatever thoughts come up but paying more attention to how they fade out of awareness. With sounds and thoughts arising and fading away there is then just the body lying in bed. See if you can let that sense fade away too, allowing the stillness and silence of night to take over. How our senses fade out at the end of each day and turn on again in the morning upon waking is as close to an everyday miracle as there is. It's worth getting interested in.

 Silent Listen

One way to get even more value out of a formal practice is to notice how quickly your mind reverts back to 'normal' at the end of the session and see what it takes to make the division between the two states that little bit more blurred. The more we pay attention to the transition between formal meditation and regular waking-life mobile meditation, the more of a chance we have of bringing the positive qualities we develop in our practice to everything we do. This particular technique is a particularly good one for learning in a formal style and then adopting when you move around. It is another technique based on a paradox and the instruction is simply to listen to silence. The natural tendency of the mind is to pay attention to the contents of the mind rather than the space around it. This technique looks to turn that around and see what happens when we do. Take some time to close your eyes, allow your back to be upright, as well as your belly soft and your face relaxed. Once you feel settled open the mind to sounds, letting the sense of hearing be the main object of awareness. And just listen. But instead of listening to the contents of sound, see if you can rest with the silence that is in between the sounds. Look even closer and see if you can notice if the silence feels more like the container for sound and that whatever sounds arise come out of it rather than being different to it. This is just a perception or way of seeing, but it is one that can encourage a real feeling of mental space. And if it makes any sense at all, see if you can hear the sound of silence. But if that doesn't mean anything to you, then don't get caught up in it. Being interested in space and silence allows our mind to be in a very different mode to its typical obsession with what's in that space or what's in that silence. Try to get a sense for what those two modes are like, how they are different and how they might be related.

 Zoom In

This is probably the formal practice I do most often. What I like about it is how it works so many different aspects of mindfulness and also has a bit of a game-like feel to it at the same time. Once we've taken some time to feel stable and settled, the practice starts by us finding a part of the body where we feel the strongest sensation. It works best if it's an area of mild tension but any clear physical sensation is fine. Gently place your attention in the area of that sensation and see if you can do what I call zooming. This means upping the resolution or magnification through which you're looking at the sensation. In other words, trying to see a higher level of detail. When we do this we will invariably notice that what at first felt like a flat sensation is actually much more than that. It unravels into a series of different sensations such as pulsing or tingling. Once we see this we settle the mind at this higher level of detail. What we might also notice is that what we first saw as tension or a pain is actually not so unpleasant when broken down into its finer details. This happens if we can flip between the level of awareness where the area is seen as a flat block and the zoomed-in level where it is seen as being made up of individual dots of sensation. Then if we like we can continue the process, zooming in on what seems like a single dot and seeing if we can resolve it into more detail. Not only does this practice refine the quality of our attention to a great extent, it also shows us that what might initially feel like a single experience can actually be much less solid than that when we look more closely. This is an important insight which we can then build on as our meditation practice develops. It is also worth knowing that practising in this way can be quite tiring and so it's worth checking to see if we're ever putting in too much energy and if we are, then just switching to a more relaxed technique like whole body breathing will allow us to settle again.

Chapter 8

The Operating System for Mobile Mindfulness

In the same way as a puppy is not just for Christmas, the practice of mindfulness should not be reserved exclusively for times of urgent need. To give ourselves the best chance of being able to access calm, kindness and balance when the stakes are the highest, we need to train in them when there is less pressure. If we only use mobile mindfulness techniques in the heat of the moment, we will see them as a sticking plaster: something we can only use on demand in urgent situations. Instead we need to approach meditation as a systematic way to cultivate positive qualities in ourselves on an ongoing basis. When we approach mindfulness in this way, we will then have the skills to deal with difficult situations and be less likely to end up in those difficult situations in the first place.

This is one of the essential ideas we need to understand if we are to get the most out of our ongoing adventures with mindfulness. Ideas are important. Supplementing all the techniques and ideas of the previous chapters, there are eight key principles which underpin the mobile mindfulness approach outlined in this book. Just as important as the techniques themselves, these principles give us the foundation and support we need to be successful.

1. Include everything

Our ambition is to train in mindfulness wherever we are, whatever we are doing. But for this style of everywhere mindfulness to truly work, we first have to believe that we can make it work at all. We need to believe that we can develop calm when we're stuck in traffic. We need to believe that we can grow our awareness in the chaos that is work; that we can develop compassion and kindness not only when dealing with our relationships and our family, but also when dealing with our inbox. We have to believe not only that change is possible, but that it is possible right here and now.

Even though faith can often be an unfashionable word, the mobile mindfulness approach does need us to have the firm belief that we can develop these positive qualities in everyday life. Even if that feels remote right now. If we don't think it is possible full stop, then we will just continue to separate our lives into parts: those parts in which we can be balanced and kind, and those parts where it is just too much. So why not at least begin with the idea that we can do it anywhere? Because unless we are open to that possibility, we don't give ourselves much of a chance in the first place.

There is no need to feel intimidated about including everything. The intention is that while everything *can*

Our ambition is to train in mindfulness wherever we are, whatever we are doing.

be part of our practice, not everything needs to be part of our practice. The point is not to become some kind of meditation superhero who is precisely aware of all experience during every waking moment of every day. The goal is simply to have the tools and the confidence to access mindfulness, irrespective of the conditions in which we find ourselves. We don't have to become a decathlete; we just need to be willing to keep fit so that when we have to run for the bus, we can.

2. Build momentum

Some benefits can be felt quickly after getting into mindfulness. In my own experience, I remember how only a few weeks after my first class, the background chatter in my mind went from being really quite noisy to really quite quiet. For you it will most probably be different. Typical early benefits of meditation can be a better quality of sleep, the ability to notice more details through our senses and a generally improved sense of steadiness or calm. All of this is wonderful but there's no need to get carried away. Since mindfulness is effectively a retraining of mental habits likely left dormant for decades, it does mean that for truly sustainable benefits we need some momentum.

Keeping up that momentum is a struggle for everyone. I haven't met a single person, myself included, who has not at some point found it a challenge to keep mindfulness a regular part of their life, even with the best of intentions. This is as true of classic formal practice as it is of this more mobile approach. Don't worry. The challenge of keeping up momentum is sort of the whole point.

Paying attention to the breath is one of the most common meditation exercises there is. The basic instruction is to place our awareness on the physical sensations of breathing where we feel them most strongly. Then when we notice that we've become distracted we just bring the mind back to the object of the breath. If our meditation was only about concentration then the measure of success would be how many breaths we're able to stick with before we get sidetracked. And while concentration is definitely worthwhile and one of the six focus themes of this book, it is awareness, not concentration, that is the most important thing. Knowing what is happening while it is happening. This knowing or noticing is absolutely key. We notice that we've become distracted and just renew the intention to come back.

Our overall relationship to meditation is exactly the same. We notice each and every time when we have lost our interest in practice, then reset our intention and go back to where we were. That resetting and going back again and again is what allows us to build up the momentum which makes mindfulness a real habit instead of just a nice idea. If we want mindfulness to be our default setting and all the positive qualities of balance, steadiness, kindness to ourselves and kindness to others to just be our natural way of being, then that momentum is absolutely key.

When hearing all this talk of momentum, it can be tempting to ask how much practice is actually enough? When people ask me this, what they tend to really mean is *What is the least amount of practice I can get away with and still get what I want?* The answer is simple: just a little bit more than you're doing right now.

3. Remember to remember

Intention is so critical to making mindfulness real. Just as with so many other things in life, before something can happen we must first want to make it happen. That wanting has to be followed up by action, but without the wanting in the first place, we won't even get off the starting blocks. That's what intention is. Without it, our energy gets scattered. With it, everything lines up.

The fact that you are reading this book at all means that you have some level of intention towards a life of greater awareness and kindness. The exercises and practices you've found here give you the means to realise that. Given that they are already designed for a time-poor life, the main challenge then becomes remembering to do them in the first place. This is solved in two ways.

The first is having a clear sense of intention. This intention might be framed in a problem-solving way: *I want mindfulness to help me fix something that's not quite working in my life*. Or it may be framed in a more positive way: *I want mindfulness to help me access a sense of space no matter what the circumstances*. Either way is fine. What is important is that we keep that motivation as close to the front of our mind as we can.

So what is your intention or your motivation right now? It might be very clear or it may not be so obvious. It is worth working out what it is. If you're not sure, then take some time to ask yourself what it is you want from mindfulness in this very moment and listen to what answers come up.

Once our intention has been set, the second way to remember to practise is to use reminders. Whenever I sit in my normal seated meditation posture with my eyes closed, my mind quickly settles down and, more often than not, my awareness becomes a little bit brighter and more vibrant than it was just a few moments before. This is not magic. It is just conditioning or learning by association. Having done a fair bit of sitting meditation over the years, my mind has associated sitting in a particular way with calm, positive mind states.

A similar thing happens when I'm walking around town. When I was starting out in mindfulness, I decided one day that whenever I saw anyone wearing a hat or something red, I would send them kind thoughts. It definitely felt a bit contrived and arbitrary to begin with but I stuck with it. Now a few years on it has become normalised as a habit. Whenever I do see someone dressed like that, spontaneous feelings of kindness and compassion just come up without my actively doing it or even thinking about it. It's such a lovely thing. And whenever it happens, any tightness I may be feeling at the time about my own particular struggles relaxes just that little bit.

This is an example of the skilful and playful use of reminders. The charging up of ordinary things around us as a way to condition us to be aware, curious and kind when we see them. Doing whatever we can to remember our intention to bring mindfulness to life. Historically, the meditation world has used things such as Buddha statues and other religious iconography as visual reminders to practise. The invitation here is to use anything and everything we can.

4. Understand how mindfulness works

The number one way to tell whether our mindfulness practice is useful or successful is by checking whether we have actually learnt anything. It is through learning about how our inner life works – its habits and its patterns – that we are able to bring more direction, space and lightness to how it all plays out.

Throughout this book you have come across dozens of different meditation exercises. Guided meditations are great and we can get an enormous amount from them. They provide the *What* – the instructions of what we need to do. However, the true magic happens when alongside the *What*, we also understand the *How* and the *Why*. Because when we know how mindfulness

works and why it works, then we are no longer just following instructions by rote, we also have the intelligence which we can then go on and deploy in any situation. There is always more we can learn from good teachers and guides, but the more we understand the mechanics, not only do we become more empowered, we become more skilled.

5. Be playful

One of the challenges of prioritising traditional sitting meditation is that many people relate to it as a chore. Just like eating a proper breakfast, it is something we know we should do, but on busy days feels like just one more thing we don't have time for. Framing meditation as a chore leads to two big problems. The first is that we can lack the motivation to do it. The second is that, even when we do manage it, we can approach it mechanically. *That's it done for another day, now what's the next thing on my to-do list?*

But what if we related to meditation not as work but as play? If we call it playfulness, fun or creativity, we can prevent our mindfulness from becoming a bit flat and protect ourselves from sabotaging new habits before we've even really begun.

The solution is simple: be creative and have fun. One of my most influential teachers once told me, 'If it's not fun, then what's the point?' It's perhaps the best advice I ever received.

So instead of doing meditation, let's play with it.

6. Don't throw out formal practice

It might be tempting to read the emphasis on real-time, mobile mindfulness as meaning that we don't need to do the old-fashioned, sitting-down, eyes-closed stuff. That is not what is being said at all.

There is something very special and important about devoting a period of time to formal meditation practice. Putting aside our other activities, sitting down, and working with a particular technique. Committing ourselves to stillness is a beautiful ritual. Even though there will inevitably be distractions, our intention is ultimately one of dedication. So even if it's only just for ten or twenty minutes, giving ourselves the gift of dedicated formal practice is a wonderful and valuable thing to do. The mindfulness tradition is built on formal sitting meditation. To ignore that would be at best negligent.

It is true that *This is Happening* does move formal sitting to a supporting role. By emphasising mobile mindfulness, I'm presenting a route into meditation that meets people where they are. This approach still very much advocates formal sitting practice as part of the overall picture. Formal meditation and mobile meditation are at their best when they work hand in hand, each reinforcing the other. As we become more skilled in accessing calm, kindness and awareness through mobile meditation, we find it easier to make time for formal sitting. As we become more experienced in formal sitting, we start to see the details of our everyday experience in higher resolution, which then unlocks new opportunities to recognise the more subtle aspects of our experience as it unfolds.

7. Make mindfulness a multiplayer game

The stereotypical image of the meditator sitting on a mountaintop, getting on with it all in splendid isolation, is common. It is also very misleading. Meditation is a social activity and always has been. Within the insight meditation tradition, it is very rare for people to have mastered the practice solely by themselves. Just as the history of mindfulness is a story of innovation and change, it is also a story of other people.

How we are on the inside affects how we express ourselves on the outside. That in turn then affects everyone around us – some a great deal and some just a tiny bit. Have you ever noticed how being in a room with very jittery people can make you more jittery? Or how you can become calmer just by spending time with someone who is themselves calm? Therefore even if you did somehow learn it all by yourself, our mindfulness practice can never be considered something that affects us in isolation.

We start to recognise the interconnectedness of our mindfulness practice more and more over time. At the beginning, we can be mainly motivated by our own stuff – our needs and our problems. This is as it should be. However, as time goes on and our practice develops and deepens, the idea of generosity and kindness to others becomes much more prominent. The mobile meditation approach takes this into account by looking to directly involve other people in the exercises and techniques we use. We've now seen how we can start to deliberately include everyone we can see around us as part of our meditation practice, using them as cues, and even targets for qualities such as gratitude and kindness.

Another aspect of the social life of meditation worth remembering is that from the earliest times up to the present day, meditation has always been something that has been done together. Given that it can be challenging at times, community has historically been absolutely vital to ensuring we have the right support and inspiration. The current range of easily accessible meditation content means that the vast majority of people now first experience meditation as something they only ever do by themselves, or in other words as a one-player game. This is a great way to begin, but I do encourage you to include some kind of social element when possible. This could be going to a class or group near you or finding an online community that looks interesting. Another good way is to find out which of your friends are interested in or have some background in mindfulness and making some time to share your experiences together.

To help encourage this idea of mindfulness as a multiplayer game, I included some practices which explicitly require you to do them with other people. Modern life can be isolating enough and it would be a shame if mindfulness were to exacerbate that feeling. Speaking to other meditators with more experience than us is also extremely valuable. It is very easy to feel that we know it all, even at the beginning of our adventures down the rabbit hole. When we spend time with wise friends and, ideally, actual experienced teachers, they will show us where we are doing well and also when we are talking nonsense.

8. Take the long view

The reason that meditators do sometimes spend time up on mountaintops is not for the isolation, it's for the views. When we spend time in nature, and especially when high up, our minds can become naturally open. There is something about having a view that is much bigger than the annoyances and challenges of day-to-day life that just helps. It literally puts things in perspective.

The same is true for time. We can put too much pressure on mindfulness when we think of it as a quick fix. Instead it is best understood as a process that has two time frames: now and later. Mindfulness is immediate and so whenever we are doing it, there is intrinsic value right there and then, right here and now. Mindfulness is also a form of training and so it is only over time that ongoing development happens. This is one of the wonderful paradoxes of mindfulness and one that works very much in our favour.

It is similar to eating well. When we eat a good healthy meal there is the pleasure and other good feelings that come with that in the moment. That single meal and its immediate positive effect also means we are more likely to continue to eat healthily in the future and so over time we can notice how our overall health improves.

Healthy eating and mindfulness are both forms of training. In fact, everything we do in one way or another is a type of training. Back in 1949, the psychologist Donald Hebb coined the now famous phrase 'neurons that fire together, wire together'. Each and every experience that we have, be that physical, emotional or mental, results in some activity in our brain cells, or neurons. If we carry out a behaviour once, that particular pattern of neural activity is reinforced once. But if we carry out the behaviour multiple times, then that pattern becomes stronger, meaning that we are more likely to be motivated to do it again. This is how behaviours become habits.

The problem is that many of our habits are mindless. As they become stronger, we become less aware of them and therefore less in control of them, resulting in the behaviour becoming automatic.

So let's do a little experiment and see what mindless habits we happen to have.

Once this sentence comes to an end, close your eyes for thirty seconds or so. Really.

Thirty seconds. No cheating.

What you have just experienced is a result of your training. If you weren't sure what you were supposed to do, you are well trained in confusion and doubt. If your mind jumped from thought to worry to planning what's for dinner, you're well trained in distraction. If you were

While it can sometimes feel like we are set in our ways forever and ever, the evidence is that our brains are constantly changing and while old habits may die hard they do die.

annoyed that I was asking you to do another exercise, then you're well trained in frustration and aversion. And if your awareness was open and relaxed, then your balance and mindfulness are in good shape.

All of these are entirely normal experiences. The reason why they are so normal is that for the past few decades of your life your mind and its attention have been kicked about by everything around us, and this has trained it to be exactly like we are right now. Even though this has been an unintentional form of training it is still training.

The good news is that our brains change. While it can sometimes feel like we are set in our ways forever and ever, the evidence is that our brains are constantly changing and while old habits may die hard they do die. *That's just how I am* just doesn't cut it, I'm afraid. Some of our habits may have developed over years and even decades, but that does not mean that it has to take that long to reverse them. There is good evidence that shows that depending on the person and the circumstances, new habits can be developed in as little as a couple of weeks. Habit reversal or development is also not an all-or-nothing process. It is not all ruined if you miss a day or two. We are also very free to mess up a little bit along the way. That is entirely normal. Having consistency over time is, however, important and so taking the longer view reminds us that habits such as mindfulness are more about the overall process than any specific instance or event.

Since change does take time, let's take the long view. If you're like me, you'll upgrade your phone every two years or so. This is a perfect time frame with which to review how your mindfulness is going. Does it have more features, more power and more functionality? Is it more beautiful, better designed and more comfortable to hold? Just as our phones improve each time we switch them up, so should our understanding and practice of mindfulness.

One more thing

Do keep an open mind. That might sound as if it goes without saying, but it is worth emphasising all the same. We all come to mindfulness for our own reasons. But as our understanding and skills develop and what we are able to see deepens, our motivations and interests may change.

Chapter 9

How to Design Your Own Meditations

While there are probably enough meditations in this book to keep you busy for quite a while, one of the reasons why I've shared so many different exercises is to give you the framework, confidence and inspiration to design your own. No one can design a mindfulness practice that fits your life as well as you can. So here is a simple guide to help you do just that.

1. **Find out which core techniques you like**
   There are six core techniques that you'll find throughout the book: body awareness, breath-based concentration, six-sense noting, knowing your attitude, loving kindness and non-doing. Give them all a go and see which ones you like and which feel most natural to you. It is always easier to make up our own meditations based on a core technique which is not only tried and tested but also that we enjoy and have an affinity for.

2. **Choose an activity that you do regularly**
   This is the context for which you'll be designing your

meditation. Popular ones you might want to try are walking, commuting, eating, cooking, working or using your phone. The key is that it's something quite ordinary to you and that it happens at a time when it's safe and OK to use your mind to meditate.

3. **Choose the quality that you want to work on**

   The previous chapters give you a good set of six to choose from: relaxation, focus, being present, balance, kindness and curiosity. You can either choose one based on an immediate need, in which case the word which fills in the gap of the sentence 'Aaargh, I really could do with some X right now' is the one to go for. Or you can choose one that is less urgent and which you just want to grow that little bit more. Both are good.

4. **Go and actually do the activity and ask yourself: how can I bring more of my chosen quality to this experience right now?**

   I can't overstate how important it is to design the practice whilst actually doing the activity you've chosen. This is the key to creating the best mobile meditations since actually being at the gym or actually being in the bath is very different to what you think being at the gym or being in the bath is like. By asking the question of how we might develop our chosen quality in that particular activity we start to see the environment in a different way, just as a designer or a researcher might do.

5. Play around with the answers you come up with

While still doing the activity, try out the different ideas that you come up with. If there's nothing that immediately springs to mind, then feel free to go ahead and give yourself a head start by looking at another meditation in the book that is for that activity or that quality. Then play around with modifying it based on what you find around you. See if you can come up with two or three different ideas and do please make them as silly or as serious as feels right.

6. Find and refine the one that works the best

Review the two or three meditation ideas that you've come up with to see which one feels best. This is normally the one that first comes to mind or the one that feels most playful or memorable. You can do this all in one go or try designing a meditation for your activity over a few goes. Then once you've got it, try adding extra elements to it or modifying it yourself. This will naturally happen over time anyway as your understanding and practice of mindfulness develops.

7. Give it a catchy name

This might sound like it is somewhat unnecessary but it's actually really important. Having a short catchy name means that the meditation you've just designed will be more memorable and if it's more memorable, then you're more likely to do it on a regular basis. The best names are two or three words long and summarise the key idea of your meditation. It's even better if the name is quite light-hearted. A good rule of thumb is that if it sounds like a mobile phone game then it's a good name.

8. **Allocate it something physical to remind you about it**

   This is another device to make your hard-won meditation memorable. Given that you've designed it for a specific activity, choose something about that activity as a visual means to remind you about it. In other words, just make the intention that whenever you next see that specific thing, be that a street sign while walking or a water bottle while at the gym, that will be a cue to do the practice. If we remind ourselves in this way enough times, it can even get to the point where you spontaneously start meditating whenever you see that thing. If we do this with enough techniques, then everything becomes a reminder for practice.

——

Worked example

Shoot Kindness is one of the mobile meditations in the chapter called *This is Connection*. This is how I designed it.

1. *Choose a core technique.* I started with the basic loving kindness practice. I actually chose it because I wasn't really getting it as a formal practice and so wanted to try using it in a different way.

2. *Choose an activity.* Walking. I walk a lot. Mainly between home and work.

3. *Choose a quality.* I wanted to make a technique that got me more involved with the people around me who I'd normally ignore.

4. *Do the activity while thinking about how to build the quality.* This bit was fun. Walking around with this question made me look at a place I thought I knew really well in a slightly different way. Thinking about how to bring other people into my awareness was also a great question for me since (I'm embarrassed to say so) it showed me how often I ignored other people as if they were just another part of the environment like a post box or bin.

5. *Play around.* This was also great fun. I remember once reading something about people playing real-life Pac-Man in a city somewhere and that got me interested in the idea of using video game ideas in real life. I fell upon the idea of shooting people kind thoughts because having played a few video games in my time, the more I paid attention to walking in the city, the more playful it felt.

6. *Find the technique that works the best.* The idea of using the kind thoughts from the loving kindness practice as something I shoot other people with actually came quite quickly. It felt like a winner right away. I did try some other variants, some of which involved me walking a bit creepily, so I quickly cut those out.

7. *Give it a name.* The idea of shooting people kindness is a very striking one and so the title was too obvious not to use.

8. *Allocate it something physical.* This was a practice I first started doing about twelve years ago and having done it so often, it's the loveliest thing when I just spontaneously start doing it. But that doesn't always happen and so what I've also done is allocate it the colour red. So whenever I see someone wearing a red coat or red top it reminds me to shoot them some kindness. It was something I chose very arbitrarily as something I'd see often but not all the time and over time it has developed into a perfect reminder.

———

Four ways to give the meditation you've designed a boost

Boost #1: Share it with someone

Try sharing the idea of your meditation with a friend and encourage them to try it. Not only can you get the satisfaction of helping someone else develop their mindfulness but they might also give you some ideas of how to refine it.

Boost #2: Do the technique as a formal practice

Take the technique that you've based your meditation on and spend some time doing it as a formal practice. When we do that, our understanding of the core technique has the chance to deepen quite significantly and the insights that you learn from your formal practice can then go on and influence your mobile mindfulness. For example, when we do the kindness practice from *This is Connection* in a formal style, we become more able to send kind thoughts to other people as we go about our day. And if we do enough formal kindness practice, those thoughts may even be spontaneous.

Boost #3: Cross-train with other techniques

While the meditation you've designed may be based on one particular core technique, do try all the others. Many of the techniques are connected in both obvious and subtle ways and having a wider set of styles in our locker means that we can up our ability to be creative.

Boost #4: Build a collection

Try and design a meditation for four or five of the main activities that you do. They might be similar meditations or they could be completely different. When we have a little collection then not only are there more times of the day when we will remember to work on our mindfulness, they will also inspire you to create more. When you do come up with some meditations of your own, there is some space in the back of the book to write them down.

Finally, and perhaps most importantly, remember to have fun. Because if it's not fun then what's the point?

Chapter 10

Generation Wise

It's easy to look back on the hippy movement of the late sixties and early seventies as a bit of a joke, now associated mainly with the drop-out stereotype and a costume you might wear to a fancy dress party when you're not particularly inspired. This would be rather unfair because some of the most progressive movements in our society today, such as environmentalism, fair trade and animal welfare can trace much of their origins back to that era. That mindfulness is where it is today and indeed the fact that you are reading this book at all is thanks to those children of the revolution.

Disillusioned by what they saw in the society and values of home and attracted by the romance of the East as advertised by George Harrison, thousands of young people travelled the so-called hippy trail over to India and then on to the rest of South and South-East Asia. While some were in it just to enjoy the trip, others were genuinely moved to explore the many spiritual traditions that they could find there. Given that the more meditative elements of Christianity had become very niche, this was an important moment since it was the first time that young Westerners in significant numbers started to be exposed to and directly train in contemplative practice.

Some of those young men and women connected deeply with what they found. Those that stayed in India ended up contributing to the development of yoga as a mainstream phenomenon and others more interested in meditative practice found their teachers in other more Buddhist countries with the insight meditation tradition of Burma, with Thailand and Sri Lanka being particularly popular, thanks to their emphasis on practicality and relative lack of pomp and ceremony.

If you want to travel to those countries today and spend some time in a meditation centre or monastery, then that is a relatively straightforward thing to do. But back in the day, conditions were much more challenging with fewer English-speaking teachers and no really well-established paths to follow. It was especially difficult for the women who made the trip since the male monastic-dominated history of Buddhist countries meant that it was that much harder to fit in. It is therefore no wonder that it is the mindfulness styles of Burma that have ended up being the most influential on the modern scene given that the Burmese meditation culture is the one with the stronger tradition of involving both women and non-monastics.

The young people that rode the hippy trail and found themselves studying mindfulness in Asia did so for different reasons. Some were hurt by a country that had gone through the Vietnam conflict and was becoming more and more led by consumerism and acquisition and were looking for other ways to orient themselves. Some had gone through their own personal trauma and were just looking for ways to deal with that. Some were excited about this thing called 'meditation' which they'd heard about but never had the chance to do themselves. Some were just going because they wanted the adventure. Whichever way they came into it, a relatively small number of the thousands that made the trip really got it. Not only did they develop a personal mindfulness practice of great benefit to themselves, but despite them still being really quite young, their Asian teachers considered them suitably gifted and experienced enough to encourage them to go back home and teach what they had learnt to others. So that's what they did.

While a handful of excellent Asian teachers had been teaching meditation in North America and Europe since the fifties, the return of the meditation pioneers from Asia meant that it was the first time ever that there was a group of non-monastic Western teachers teaching mindfulness to non-monastic Western students in the West. That was kind of a big deal. As the young American and European audience tended to be more interested in the practical mind-training over the more esoteric, ritual and religious elements of Buddhism, it was meditation that was given priority rather than a wider religious system. This was also a big deal. Meditation was now decoupled from the wider Buddhist package and was its own thing. However, since the young teachers had learnt mindfulness primarily as a spiritual practice, that is how they taught it. But what happened next changed everything.

Mindfulness started to get remixed. This happened in three ways. The first was that unlike before when meditation teachers would be steeped only in one tradition, this generation of teachers had trained in a variety of styles and the meditation they taught was different as a result. Back in Asia it basically never happened that a Zen teacher would meet a teacher from Burma or Tibet. But now all these different styles were meeting each other for the first time and it was creating new understanding. The second way in which mindfulness began to change was that people came along to give it a go who didn't care too much for the spiritual aspects. Instead they were more interested in solving their own particular problems and just making their days that little bit better. This was the start of people picking and choosing the bits of mindfulness they liked and leaving out the bits they didn't think were quite for them. The third way in which mindfulness got remixed was that people who studied it for their own very personal reasons started to think about how it might be applied to other situations and contexts with which they were familiar. The most significant instance of this was how members of those early practice communities who also happened to work in healthcare then went on to apply mindfulness training to clinical and therapeutic contexts, and thereby accelerated the boom in mindfulness we see today.

As a long-time student not only of mindfulness itself but also of its history, I am forever indebted to that small group of pioneering teachers. After training in Asia, they came back home and taught a translated and remixed version of meditation that has gone on to be the foundation for the modern mindfulness movement as we know it today. While they themselves certainly stood on the shoulders of giants, anyone who has got anything out of mindfulness in the last thirty or forty years stands on theirs. I have had the good fortune to meet some of them in recent years, and they readily admit that they had no idea what they were doing in those early days. But in the days and years that followed, with great skill, patience and personality they shepherded mindfulness to where it is today.

The history of mindfulness is one of evolution and change. If you want to understand how mindfulness has evolved, then there's only one idea you need to know and it is one that has already been mentioned: when mindfulness moves to a new place, it changes in response to the traditions that it finds there. The tradition that mindfulness met for the first time when it moved from Asia to North America and Europe was science. It is that meeting of meditation and science, in particular neuroscience, psychology and psychotherapy, that has been the most significant in the last few decades.

So what's next? While the influence of that original golden generation of Western mindfulness teachers will continue to be felt, we are now seeing the emergence of an entirely new mindfulness generation. It is a generation of people who will never travel to Burma to learn meditation in a monastery. Nor will they be that interested in the more spiritual elements. Instead this is a generation of people who want to learn mindfulness on their own terms and apply it to the places where they are, even if those are places where mindfulness has never gone before. This can be in a small way such as working out how to bring more mindfulness to our office or when we're doing the school run. Or it can be in a much grander way such as working on how to make mindfulness part of the culture of a whole business or education system. I call it 'Generation Wise'. And you're part of it.

When I started this book, my one overriding hope was that people would become excited about this idea of designing their own meditations. For me that is when mindfulness becomes a truly creative practice. We can learn a general technique and approach but it is only when we work out how to adapt it to the vagaries and challenges of our own mind and our own life that it starts to make a real difference.

Whether you call it adaptation, change or innovation, it has been a key part of mindfulness since the very beginning. So if you do start to build a practice and take what you've learnt and tweak it a little so that it works better for you, then you will be in good company. I'm excited for you and I'm excited about where mindfulness itself may go next. More and more of us are making the decision to look inside and build our inner resources in response to the challenges that we face, both big and small. What might our worlds look like if we valued our inner resources as much as we do our outer ones?

Something is happening. Now that the mindfulness cat is out of the spiritual bag, the ideas and practices are starting to spread into places they have never been before. Mindfulness changes us. That is sort of the whole point. So the more people engage with it and the more diverse those types of people are, the wider that change will be. While I don't necessarily see a world where everyone becomes a regular meditator, I do see one in which those of us interested in having more awareness and kindness in our societies take what we learn from mindfulness and apply that to the wider contexts in which we live and work. I happen to be a designer and maker of technologies and so that is the world where I express my understanding of mindfulness. You may be a teacher or a manager or a nurse or an accountant. You may be a father or a mother. The invitation for you is the same: how can you best express your own understanding in the places where you find yourself?

While mindfulness is part of many of the great various contemplative traditions, the original roots of mindfulness as a systematic practice are to be found in early Buddhism. This was back in ancient India the best part of three thousand years ago where the biggest city around was what today we would consider a small town and the most advanced piece of technology going was a plough. So while the original tradition is full of key information and insight, it would be a mistake to assume that a system designed for that particular time would automatically have all the answers for the world as we know it today. The Buddha didn't have an iPhone. Nor indeed did those original teachers, although some of them do now. The world has changed so much in the last forty years and, if anything, that change seems to accelerate all the time. To remain relevant, mindfulness itself has to change again.

We are starting to see the practices and ideas of mindfulness influence everything from healthcare to celebrity culture.

In this chapter we're going to go on a whistle-stop tour of six different ways in which mindfulness is changing not only the world but itself and meet some of the people who are helping make that happen. And given that it's been such a key theme of the book so far, let's start with technology.

———

Mindfulness and the machine

The retreat is historically a very important part of most meditation traditions, including those most closely related to modern mindfulness. It is a time when we remove ourselves from the outside world and dedicate ourselves to looking inside. The emphasis on the retreat model was a key part of the approach that that pioneering group of early teachers brought back to our shores and the great rural meditation centres that they started back in the seventies and eighties continue to help a lot of people to this day.

I'm always a little bit saddened by how many people I meet who think that retreat is the only way of dealing with technology. *Mindfulness is all about slowing down*, they tell me, *and technology is all about speeding up. Therefore mindfulness has nothing to do with technology. So the only thing to do is turn it all off.* I do agree that taking a break from our devices can be very useful. But just as going on holiday is not a very sensible strategy for dealing with a difficult work situation, if we are finding aspects of our digital life challenging then turning everything off is not the answer. Turning it all off and going off grid is also not sustainable. Our lives are increasingly based around using digital tools and services and while some of us may be able to afford to change that entirely, the rest of us neither have that luxury nor would even want to. When dealing with all the pressures of digital life, the retreat move isn't a particularly sophisticated one but while I am saddened every time I hear it, it doesn't surprise me. Not only is the idea of retreat still so embedded in how people understand mindfulness, that key generation of senior teachers is not particularly digital literate. If someone is struggling to get their TV to work properly, I wouldn't expect them to have the most progressive point of view on mindfulness in a digital age.

So if retreat is only part of the answer, what else is there? Digital life has been a key theme throughout the book and all the technology-related exercises have been in service of changing our relationship with our devices and what they do. The key to mindfulness is understanding that while we may not always be able to do anything about what is happening, we do have a choice about how we relate to it. We've explored that in the context of things like difficult emotion and what is happening in our bodies, but the very same thing applies to our devices. As users of all this technology we have the opportunity to stop demonising our phones and our news feeds and instead start relating to them all as devices of wellbeing. This may sound like a tall order, and in some cases it may well be, but just as with changing our relationship with our inner critic, the prize is so worth it. And mindfulness can help.

There is a third strategy in helping us live a life with both mindfulness and technology and just like retreat and working

As users of all this technology we have the opportunity to stop demonising our phones and our news feeds and instead start relating to them all as devices of wellbeing.

on the relationship, it also starts with an R: redesign. Because it is true that our technologies are having an impact on our attention and therefore the quality of our wellbeing. But the key thing to know is that the problem is not technology per se; the problem is bad technology.

We've already looked at how free-with-advertising is the business model which has won the web. This means that one of the main jobs of the designers, engineers, psychologists and behavioural experts that currently work on our apps and websites is to make sure we click the ad or make the in-app purchase. Whether it's games or social networks or news sites, which is where we spend the vast majority of our screen time, they are literally designed to increase our distraction or addiction. Currently the metrics which are prioritised are things like advertising click-through and revenue per user. What if those responsible for making our products also included qualities such as self-awareness and kindness? What might our digital world look like if they did?

I make my living by making mindfulness apps, and while there definitely has been a bit of a boom in recent years, the industry is still very much in its infancy. The clearest sign of this for me is how most of what is out there is in some way based on guided audio meditation exercises. Guided audio is not only a relatively limited form for getting the most out of what mindfulness has to offer but it is also a twentieth-century technology. A large part of my motivation for writing this book is to bring more creativity and innovation to the mindfulness conversation. Despite innovation being so key to its history, much of how mindfulness is presented and understood is relatively conservative. While guided audio exercises can be a very effective way of introducing people to mindfulness, an unintended consequence of them being so dominant is that we are creating a generation of meditators who can only do it with their headphones on. That is not very empowering. It is therefore a challenge for companies such as mine to invent and share new ways of bringing mindfulness to life. Again, like all the opportunities explored in this chapter, this is already happening. There is an emerging group of companies across the world working on so-called contemplative technologies which use everything from brainwave sensors to game design as a way to make a wider range of products in service of better inner wellbeing.

This is all great. But it does miss a big opportunity. The growth of specialist apps and gadgets that have mindfulness 'on the tin' is definitely a win. But the *epic* win is stitching mindfulness into all of our technologies. There are currently no departments for mindful design in companies such as Facebook, Google, Samsung, Apple or Netflix. But if there were, then including even a tiny aspect of mindfulness into a mass-market product, be that software or hardware, would have a massive impact. What's more, as we become more literate in how our attention works, there will come a time when we consumers are no longer OK about how much it is being bullied. The last fifty years of the fair trade movement have shown how there is a market for ethical products and that we care about the impact of what we consume. The opportunity we have for the next fifty years is to do for our minds what we have done for Costa Rican coffee farmers and, if possible, do it at a scale where it impacts all technology users not just a small elite who can afford to pay a premium. If we don't, then we can have all the mindfulness apps and books that we like, but it'll only ever be window dressing rather than the real change we need.

I, however, am an optimist. Not only that, I am also a technoptimist. All of which means that I can see a world in which our software and our hardware are designed to be mind-positive. I see bestselling games which are won by compassion rather than killing. I see popular news sites which support our depth of concentration instead of bombarding us with ads. I see everyday domestic appliances which quietly remind us to be present in how we're feeling. This is currently happening in pockets but it will grow. Mindfulness is being practised by more and more people and some of them are the very people who make our technologies. As their practice and understanding matures they will see that using meditation only to support their own

Redesign will take some time so while it does, what we can do as individuals is use our influence where we can and work on our own personal relationship with technology.

wellbeing is not enough, and that they have the power to impact billions of people through the products they work on. We now have the tools to measure wellbeing in ways that we've not been able to before and therefore it is only a matter of time before our giant tech companies get interested in how their products can make our lives happier as well as more efficient. Because those same tools might also be used to show the negative impact of those same products, and the popular technology industry could then find itself in the same situation as the tobacco industry and no one wants that to happen. Redesign will take some time so while it does, what we can do as individuals is use our influence where we can and work on our own personal relationship with technology.

———

A kinder office

One of the reasons I'm so optimistic that our digital world will become more influenced by mindfulness is that many of the people who make it are now meditators. In an echo back to the seventies, where many of the leading lights in the area which would go on to be known as Silicon Valley were never that far away from the counter-culture, mindfulness is now being practised and taught in many start-ups as well as large household-name technology companies. And considering that one of the things that the technology world revolves around is data, it has been the findings of all the mindfulness research in the last twenty years which have given mindfulness enough legitimacy as something which can get corporate sign-off as a way to support both employee wellbeing and productivity. If it was the data that helped adoption by the tech industry that gave mindfulness in the workplace its way in, this very adoption has resulted in even more. Because corporate senior managers do love the argument, 'If Google do it, then maybe we should do it too.'

It has been fascinating to watch the growth of workplace mindfulness in the last ten years. Back when I first started meditating, I was working in a classic office environment and even then I could see how wellbeing was becoming something that companies of all shapes and sizes were starting to pay real attention to. While I'm just an observer, Louise Chester knows this world inside out. For the last five years Louise has been working with a range of companies to bring mindfulness to their employees. When we met, she told me about how she first became interested in mindfulness as a teenager but only really started practising properly twenty years ago as a way to help her deal with a bereavement. Louise subsequently spent many successful years working in finance, which culminated in a very senior role for an international fund manager.

I found my mindfulness practice to be the most incredible gift. It helped me have more balance in all areas of my life, including what was a high-pressure career. Then six years ago, I began to notice how much more new evidence was being published on the measurable benefits of mindfulness practice and it inspired me to start a new career. I had gained so much myself and I was moved to help other people who were working in the kind of challenging work environments which I knew so well.

One of the main concerns I have about workplace mindfulness is that it becomes perceived purely as a productivity tool, using attentional training to help people become less distracted and doing so in a somewhat cynical way without perhaps looking at the more structural issues as to why people aren't so focused on their work. I was, however, encouraged by what Louise had to say.

It's true that some companies are more interested in mindfulness as a way to boost productivity and some are more motivated by overall employee wellbeing. But whichever way you come to mindfulness training, ultimately the benefits meet, since you can't achieve your full potential if you are suffering from debilitating levels of stress. What works best is when mindfulness is introduced from the bottom up as well as the top down. Interest starts to build organically within an organisation once a small group of people have tried it out. And there's a real boost when members of senior management do the training and coaching programmes and publicly acknowledge great benefits. This gives mindfulness that extra bit of credibility. We've seen the best long-term results where mindfulness moves from being a one-off training course into a core aspect of an organisation's learning and development, leadership and wellbeing programmes.

While the idea of mindfulness may be a bit too left field for some companies, there has been a real rise in its adoption over the last few years. That is in part due to the scientific validation behind mindfulness but there are other factors. If companies want to attract and retain talent, reduce risk and environmental impact, increase their responsibility as an organisation in the world and still sustain healthy economic returns, they need to embrace the idea of being a more conscious business. When done well, mindfulness training can be a key tool in making that change.

When I asked Louise about the future, she was very clear about where workplace mindfulness can go next. *My hope is that as workplace mindfulness matures, organisations not only focus on productivity and attention but also start to emphasise the aspect that is all about kindness and compassion. When we are in an environment that doesn't feel benevolent or compassionate then even if we have the attentional skills, it is hard to access them. So many workplaces are full of fear, reactivity or egotism and we end up being defensive, just doing whatever we can to keep ourselves safe and get through. To be at our best, we need to operate within a culture of cooperation and mutual support. Up to this point, corporate mindfulness training has tended not*

*to emphasise that aspect as much, but mindfulness training
is a fantastic tool for building cultures of kindness, that help
employees to thrive and be their best selves. I think organisations
are coming round to acknowledging that 'good' business is good
business and the best way of creating long-term sustainable
corporate success.*

Healing the mind

Work can definitely be stressful, but it is another thing
entirely to have the kind of difficulties that lead to being
diagnosed with conditions such as anxiety and depression.
The increasing prevalence of mental health issues is well
known yet those conditions continue to be stigmatised in
a way that more obviously physical health conditions do
not. Much of the data leading to the adoption of workplace
mindfulness has actually come from research into its clinical
application. Mindfulness as the basis of therapy began as
an idea in the mid-seventies and has since developed in a
clinically recognised and recommended intervention for
specific conditions. Having always worked in the area of 'pop
mindfulness', the more clinical aspects of mindfulness are
not something I know first-hand. So to help me understand
where it might go next, I went to see Chris O'Sullivan. Chris
holds a senior role in a major mental health charity in the
UK. You've actually met him before. He was the Chris who
just happened to be on the scene of that awful lorry crash in
Glasgow city centre and stepped in to help the injured.

Out of all the people I spoke to for this chapter, Chris is perhaps the person who has got into mindfulness the most recently. While he has been following it for several years as part of his work, it wasn't actually until very recently that he deliberately started practising it for himself. *I'd gone through a lot of personal upheaval and change in recent times. I'd been unwell, lacked energy, had a lot of doubt, we'd just had our first child and I was at a key phase of my career. There was just so much happening and I recognised the herald of impending burn-out. I had read about some of the mindfulness evidence, some of the critique, and some of the mindfulness books that people like me buy at airports when on business trips. It made a certain amount of sense and after giving it a go I found the practices fascinating and compelling. It ended up really helping me navigate what was a challenging time.*

Like many people who love their work I often find I have no off switch. For years I devoured opportunities to do more, prove myself to myself, show the bullied teenager I once was that carrying on was worth something. My work came before looking after myself. Then I became a father, and the axis shifted. Having a child pulled on my reserves of mental and physical resilience, but was a wonderful reason to force a reframing.

Mindfulness has helped me in a range of ways. First is that I've become aware of the extent to which I was absorbed in my own narrative, needs and, on occasion, negativity. I've been able to use techniques to help manage my energy levels and modu-late my relationships at work, especially in times of challenge. It's made me more deliberate and improved my decision-making and strategic thinking by enabling me to non-judgementally listen to others and examine my motivations. I've also realised how much I've taken for granted. I've stopped buying things just to make me feel happy and realised that a free day in the garden with my family matters more. I've realised that what I have to offer them is enough, and that often at work what's good enough is good enough. I've learnt to fail, and to enjoy change, and the possibilities it brings.

The opportunity to meditate when out and about has also increased my level of physical activity. And now that I'm into the kindness techniques, I have noticed that I am far less judgemental, even internally, and more prepared to notice and acknowledge other people's states, positions and motivations without rising to bait or responding defensively. That has made me more level-headed at work and at home, and a better manager of people and crises. I have found a way to reorganise and reframe my work life, and delight in the fatherhood of two small children. I'm sure that mindfulness has helped that personal resilience.

I can't be 100 per cent sure that mindfulness did all of this. Looking back it was probably a mixture of things – mindfulness, my love of photography, my family, my work and just life. But what it has done is help me reconnect to the things I already had but had lost sight of.

As both a relative newbie to meditation and someone who has a professional understanding of the mental health world, I was keen to get Chris's perspective on why mindfulness has grown so much and where it might go next. The first factor he highlighted as to why it has come to be such a popular treatment for mental health conditions is that it works. *It helps people whose thoughts are chaotic to bring a sense of order, peace and calm to their lives.*

Mindfulness makes a lot of sense as an adjunctive therapy, which means it's used alongside another type of main intervention. Whilst not entirely risk-free for everyone at every time in their life, the seeds of the technique can be nurtured in some ways by almost everybody. It has therefore got a favourable risk profile compared with other interventions. Mindfulness is something a person can take control of and responsibility for. It cannot be done to you or against your will. It therefore fits well with self-management strategies and with the concept of recovery.

Finally, mindfulness can be relatively well researched through trials, and there is growing interest in mindfulness research in leading institutions. The robust evidence base for self-management and self-help strategies is sparse but it is growing, and when mindfulness shows potential it is easier for policy makers and research funders to get involved.

As to where it goes next, mindfulness is certainly in the public eye now and rightly so. The area I'm most interested in both personally and professionally is access. How can mindfulness work for the people who most need support but who are the furthest from the places where mindfulness currently reaches? As a white middle-class man with access to technology and a good social circle, it's easy for me to get access to mindfulness as it is now. The challenge for the future is how mindfulness changes and evolves to help different types of people. And as a father, I'm also excited about the prospect of how mindfulness has a great potential to support young people and their parents. It may not be the solution for everything but it's a hugely useful skill for navigating modern life.

Education from the inside out

Chris's wish to see mindfulness develop into something that reaches more disadvantaged people as well as children made me go and see Michael Bready. Michael is based just a short walk away from my house in Glasgow and I have followed his work with both interest and no small amount of admiration. Michael and his team work with children and teachers all in service of the belief that mindfulness and the ability to look inside will help young people lead more healthy, happy and compassionate lives. He is also involved in some special projects, with the one that I find most fascinating being a two-year piece of research in which he teaches mindfulness in Scotland's largest young offenders' institution to young men between the ages of eighteen and twenty-one. It is amazing work but when I meet Michael for coffee, I was interested to know how he got into mindfulness in the first place. I found out that it was because a girl broke his heart when he was eighteen years old. Talk about silver linings.

I think I would have always got into the practice at some point but it was the heartbreak that was the catalyst. I think it was the first time I had really experienced suffering. It stopped me in my tracks and made me think, woah, what is this? That led me to become interested in another way of living, to be curious about how I could cultivate a sense of real strength.

I didn't want to have a hard shell, but I wanted to develop a solidity within myself and still live fully and wholeheartedly. It was while I was thinking all this that I became aware of meditation and thought, hey, maybe there's something in that.

I started reading ancient philosophy and became interested in humanistic psychology but for all the beautiful ideas I felt like I needed a practice – some way to actually cultivate the habits of mind and being that all these philosophers said were so important. So I took a meditation course in Glasgow, began reading a lot on the subject and it became something that never went away. When I was about twenty-four I went travelling to India. I thought I would spend a lot of time doing the tourist thing but ended up practising in monasteries for about nine months.

I assumed that Michael had then worked as a teacher and that is what had led to him working with schools but it wasn't quite as straightforward as that. After his Asian travels he went to the United States to complete a master's degree in positive psychology and was inspired by the many different programmes that existed for school children and students related to wellbeing, mentoring and entrepreneurship.

It made me wonder what could be done to enhance young people's wellbeing at a much bigger level? That is what led me to education. Education is changing but many of its aims have not changed for the best part of 150 years. The traditional academic elements are vitally important but there has to be a broader purpose now.

I used to think that wellbeing had to be given greater priority alongside these traditional goals but I now believe that wellbeing is not just an aspect of education, but its fundamental purpose. What we all want is for our young people to be healthy, happy, flourishing individuals and part of a healthy, happy, flourishing society. Everything we do in schools should be in service of enabling that, but so much of the time we get obsessed with the instrumental means to that end. We get obsessed with exams, academic achievement or challenging bad behaviour and then sacrifice the ultimate end – the young person's wellbeing.

So yes, it's good that people like me are taking steps in the direction of making wellbeing more important but I think what we actually need to do is change the fundamental nature of education so that schools can become places for healing and transformation. Lots of kids, even young kids, have already experienced suffering and trauma and so we should be creating environments that help them heal – and at the very least don't make things worse. Further still, we should be enabling all kids, irrespective of their upbringing, to cultivate the habits of being that will help them throughout life such as kindness, courage, honesty, joy and gratitude. That's my hope at least.

Michael teaches courses for children as young as eight years old up to young adults as well as running courses for existing school teachers to add mindfulness to their repertoire. I was keen therefore to get a sense for how schools and the children themselves find it.

The reception is always extremely positive. The interest of the education world is a reflection of the overall enthusiasm for mindfulness that is happening across the media and across the whole of society. Ultimately it's because we're just all perpetually stressed out. We are working too hard. We are all trying to earn more money. The question then becomes why? What's the point given that it's not really bringing us more happiness? My take is that the growth of mindfulness is attributable to our forgetting how to be happy and where actual happiness lies. That's just as true for the world of education as it is for society as a whole.

One of the hardest things about teaching mindfulness to young kids, when compared to adults, is that kids haven't yet realised that life is actually pretty tough. When adults come to mindfulness, they're often world-weary, struggling to cope and looking for something that can bring relief. As I said before, some kids have had very tough times but a lot of young kids have a natural zest and vitality – a joy in living. To start off talking about the suffering that comes with life is just a bit of a drag and doesn't connect. So, when teaching younger kids, instead of presenting mindfulness as a way to solve problems, it's all about making it fun and tapping into their natural curiosity. If you can come up with ways for them to be really interested in what's happening in their mind, what's happening in their body, and what's happening in their experience from moment to moment, that is the best way to bring them into the practice.

When it comes to the young offenders it's very different. In conventional classrooms there are norms of behaviour, which makes teaching easier. But young offenders will resist and rebel against anything that seems like a school lesson. The key is to connect with them on a human level first. I can talk endlessly about the benefits of mindfulness, the theory and the neuroscience, but these guys are just not interested in that. The first thing is to make sure they feel safe with me, that I'm all right. If I'm an *all right guy, then they are more willing to give what I'm saying a shot.*

The other major difference from teaching young children is that many of these young men have a great deal of suffering in them. Mindfulness asks us to be really honest with what's happening inside us and, like anyone else, there's resistance to accepting that there is suffering, let alone looking at it. So it can take some time to get going. But once they go through the course and start to develop the practice, they discover many benefits: they don't get so angry, they feel more relaxed, they sleep better, they get into fewer fights. I'm always so impressed and even over-awed by their courage. These guys have some intense stuff inside them and they still sit. It's so inspiring to see the strength of the human spirit in being present to even the most difficult things.

As I close my conversation with Michael I ask him about what he's most excited about for the next few years. He is quick to answer. *Whether it's in the classroom or in prisons or in companies or just in your front room, mindfulness gives us something to do to improve our lives. I often do short presentations on mindfulness and participants will often only understand it intellectually. But when I teach longer courses, the deeper experiential understanding emerges. It's amazing to see how so many different types of people are now moving mindfulness from a nice idea into something that's really alive. The boom in interest is all driven by what people are feeling and experiencing on the inside. That's why they talk about it to others and that is how it spreads organically. They talk about how it's changed their life, about how it's helped them become more human. So what I'm excited about is that happening to more people.*

The power of outside

As shown by Michael's moving work, mindfulness has gained so much in the last few years. Something it has perhaps lost, however, is its relationship with nature and the outdoors. Since the very earliest times in its history, mindfulness-based meditation has been something done outside. That has not only been because it grew up as a tradition in places with warm climates but also because nature can be a teaching environment in its own right. That is why I was excited to meet Andres Roberts who spends much of his time supporting people to develop their relationship with nature, work which is very much informed by his own practice and understanding of mindfulness. What got him going was his passion for changing the world.

I started working for a big bank straight out of university. It was at an exciting time in the art scene in London and so much was happening. Installation art was becoming a big thing, as was participative theatre and some of the festivals that are massive today were just beginning to take off. It made me feel like I was split in two since my work looked so different when compared to the energy of all that. I just thought, wow, why is it that organisations like the bank I was at are so restrictive? I saw how the cultures and structures that organisations set up make so many people shut themselves off from being wholly themselves. They just turn up at work, step into a job description and only really come alive again at five o'clock, in the pub or at the weekend. It was that experience which got me really interested in the whole idea of changing organisations for the better, making them more human.

What got me into mindfulness was the realisation that
before you can make any positive change happen out in the
world you need to work on yourself. That led me to explore dif-
ferent ways of doing that and it was during this time that I came
across a well-known mindfulness teacher who has since been
very influential. He talks about three nested circles. The smallest
one represents you, the middle one represents your close group of
family and friends, and the largest circle represents your wider
organisation or society as a whole. One of the parts of his teach-
ing that has really stuck with me is that before you do anything,
you need to bring yourself home, back to that inner circle. It was
curiosity that led me into mindfulness rather than any particu-
lar crisis and my first experience of practising in nature was
in Spain when a friend of mine who was working there helped
me do my first solo. A solo is a period of time you spend alone
without any external distractions and with no other instructions
than to be in nature and be interested in what happens.

My first solo was twenty-four hours and it was perhaps
the first time in which I was able to look inside myself in a
completely different way. Interestingly enough it was raining. It
rained quite a lot through those twenty-four hours which meant
I had to sit underneath this tiny sheet of tarpaulin with a small
fire nearby. But I was happy as could be. I was at the top of this
mountain overlooking this incredible valley. There was a real
sense of adventure. Sitting there, I hit on this place of stillness
which allowed me to hear, for the first time, where some of my
inner voices came from.

One of the inner voices I remember listening to was one
I call the Broadcaster. The Broadcaster is the impulse to say

something. No matter what, it interrupts whatever is happening to express its opinion and give its two penny's worth. It's a bit uncomfortable with silence and so just chats away. It was the first time that I saw it in detail, so when I recognised it I gave it that name. In that solo, I must have noticed seven or eight different kinds of internal voice. It was quite an education and made me want to not only learn more about mindfulness in nature but also to help other people have their own experiences.

Speaking to Andres made me want to pack a bag and run into the countryside and I was keen to get his sense about what it is about nature that means it does what it does. While he found it hard to boil it down to one thing, the thing he did emphasise was how healing it is. He told me about a practice in Japan and Korea called 'forest bathing'. Forest bathing is going for a walk in the forest on a regular basis over a number of weeks. There's no deep meditative aspect to it in particular; it is just spending time in nature with the intent of being well and taking care of yourself. And it's been shown how being in nature can trigger all sorts of positive responses. Forest bathing does sound lovely and gentle but it did make me ask Andres if people find the intensity of the solos that he helps facilitate hard at all.

Not everyone is ready for the more remote solos and so we do run more gentle ones such as in the middle of an organic farm which, while still beautiful, is not really very wild. We do that deliberately so as to support people who haven't camped before or who are a little bit scared of being alone, being in the dark or of something so physical. What people tend to discover is that most of the fears they have coming in are constructed before the

solo and when they actually do it the reality is that they are
more than capable of dealing with it. People recognise that they
have much more potential than they think and are capable of
really amazing things. In fact, many people go into a solo a little
hesitantly and then afterwards say that they want another day
or two.

Interest in the wild and in nature is definitely growing.
Obviously there are the concerns around climate change and the
need to become more aware of our environment. But alongside
that there is also the fact that the reasons we need stillness and
space are growing enormously. I was recently with a team of
people in their early twenties and they told me that lots of their
friends had experienced anxiety at that very early age. I'm in
my late thirties and I don't remember that happening when I
was twenty. Sometimes we need that stillness just to know how
we're doing.

Teaching fluidity

Mindfulness is changing and growing so much that there
are dozens of people that I could have spoken to with all
sorts of experiences and perspectives on what is happening
and where it might all go next. Generation Wise is made
up of so many different types of people who are all looking
inside and working out how what they discover can be
best expressed. We've seen how mindfulness started as a
spiritual practice to help people see some quite profound
things about what it is to be alive and aware and how it has

since evolved to be so much more than that. So to finish my whistle-stop tour of the ways in which mindfulness is changing I went to meet two people who understand the depth of meditation but also the fluidity of how it is moving and shifting better than anyone I know.

Emily and Vincent Horn are both meditation teachers who also run a popular podcast series, conference and website all about the past, present and future of Buddhism. They happen also to be husband and wife and, at the time of writing, the parents of a brand-new human being. Vincent grew up in a family of people interested in spirituality and his first experience of meditation was through a class that his aunt was teaching at her house when he was just thirteen. It was through this friendly kind of family peer pressure that he first became introduced to the idea of using his mind to explore his mind. This original spark led to a lifelong adventure of serious meditation practice and study. Emily started dating Vincent while they were both undergraduates at university and she first tried meditation using some insight meditation CDs that Vince had in his room. She felt an instant connection with the practice and she says that it seemed to nurture a sense that she'd had from a young age that perhaps life wasn't all that she made it out to be. She became passionate about knowing how her mind worked as well as using it to find some relief from her day-to-day stress.

Over time their practice developed and they became meditation teachers in their own right. Emily often teaches in traditional retreat centres, while Vince works with individual students as well as technology start-up teams who want to begin using mindfulness. Vince told me how he comes across two different kinds of people. *Some people want to go quite deep and then there are those who really want to just develop certain skills and aren't so interested in the deeper aspects. I've seen how there's been an increase in the number of the second type of person in the last couple of years. For them, mindfulness is very practically oriented, asking questions like* How do I apply this right away?

However, the division between what we're calling deep and everything else isn't so big. It's mainly a function of time and attention. When people up the dosage of how much they're meditating, especially in formal practice, they start uncovering more subtle layers of the mind that they didn't have the ability to see before. When you move from doing ten minutes of formal practice to doing half an hour then you will naturally start having new insights.

Emily has also noticed how fluid it can be between the more traditional ways of approaching meditation and the much more modern. *One of the biggest changes I have seen is in the amount of people who turn up to retreat centres that have first been introduced to meditation through apps. People seem more inclined towards mindfulness practice than ever before, so it brings up an interesting cultural question at these centres which can, for various reasons, be a little bit anti-technology. It also raises questions about how we actually teach. For example, how do we as teachers support people in training their hearts and minds in a way that is both as universal as an app, but personal at the same time, given that historically a big role* of teachers and mentors is to help guide people in their own individual territory?

Something modern mindfulness definitely does have a larger number of today is more diverse female voices. I was keen to get Emily's perspective on how meditation is changing from its traditional past which tended to be dominated by male teachers. She felt that the most important thing is that people hear the understanding of mindfulness expressed through a female voice. *Our tone, stories, and way of explaining can only augment the male-centred history of meditation. Teachers that lean more towards the feminine have the opportunity to bring forth different kinds of emphasis such as tending to others, to relationships, or observing rhythms and cycles. Throughout history women have included spiritual practice as part of their lives. We haven't been as apt to leave our homes and families as men. Basket weaving, planting the fields, rocking our children – these are ample opportunities for meditation and the cultivation of concentration and presence. It is important, though, that the feminine is empowered to come through not only women but also men, and that women are able to express themselves in a way that doesn't just mimic what has gone before.*

Alongside the growing diversity of voices, I am also personally really curious about how and where mainstream mindfulness overlaps the more spiritual aspects. I am excited to find new ways of integrating the sacred so that people have a fullness in their lives without feeling like it belongs to religion. But how do we do that without throwing the baby out with the bathwater? There is a happiness and sacredness that comes from the deeper

aspects of practice. Ideally we should aim to include the medita-
tion approaches which shy away from spiritual baggage.

The meditation trends that Vince is most excited about revolve around new technology, in particular what he calls 'technodelics', a name taken from an article written by his friend Jason Lange to mean technologies being explicitly developed to help people experience states of consciousness that they normally don't have access to. *These so-called 'tech-nodelics' will therefore have the potential to introduce people to the kinds of experiences that can happen in deep meditation but without them actually having to meditate. Unlike the stigmas that exist around mind-altering substances, there will be a lot less resistance to strapping on a headset compared to taking an illegal drug. It makes me wonder if there might be a cultural impact even bigger than the hippy movement on the horizon with these technologies where Grandma puts on a headset and suddenly her whole mind is blown and she experiences herself as something completely different from who she normally is.*

The idea of Grandma having her mind blown does somewhat worry me and Vince shares that concern with regard to the potential risks. *There will no doubt be negative side effects such as the potential of addiction or the inability to handle dissociation from your normal reality. This already happens with meditation in some cases. Sometimes people have an experience or even many experiences where they have a real profound moment that seems to be different from their ordinary experience and then they get in this habit of trying to get back there and feeling like there's something wrong when they're not there. Then meditation becomes a tool that is used to escape* reality. I think that technodelics have even more potential to do that and so we need to look out for that.

The other main concern I have about mindfulness is that in all the excitement, we forget the importance of other people. Most of the current research into mindfulness tends to reduce things down to what is happening in the brains of individual people after doing certain techniques. We're in a cultural moment where we want everything to be quantifiable. Meditation practice clearly has an effect on the brain but so too does a relationship with a mentor or teacher or a wider community. We need to remember that otherwise it would be a massive loss.

When I ask Emily if she has any concerns about how mindfulness is growing, she points to the fact that *as individuals, we have to be as smart as possible about what we get into. There are always benefits and weaknesses to any approach or method. There are also more and less skilled people teaching all kinds of things. Whether it's mindfulness, yoga or anything else, we have to develop the ability to trust our own experience and work out what is appropriate for us.*

Finally, I couldn't leave them without asking about what it is like as long-term deep meditators to have recently become new parents. Vince told me how as a father he certainly feels like his heart is opening more. *I'm developing a greater patience and not taking the more challenging things such as him screaming in the middle of the night so personally. I can definitely see some real benefits in that we're having to go through some things that I'd never choose to put myself through and that is forcing both of us to develop in certain ways. It doesn't always feel good but that's usually how most development happens.*

It happens out of tension and out of friction and out of challenge. In that sense I can definitely feel there's some growth happening!

Emily agrees. *Becoming a parent has been one of the most challenging and rewarding experiences of my life. The whole process from the moment I found out I was pregnant to the second he first cried and now to the everyday care is a reflection of what I have learnt through my meditation practice. There are ups and downs, cycles and stages, selfish and selfless action. I am learning that practice seeps through every moment and when I am not fully present with my son, he lets me know almost instantly. There are times when I don't want to get up at 2 a.m. or change his nappy again. Yet I'm able to let that sense of myself arise and pass away while responding to the needs of another being. He reminds me that a part of me is developing by itself and requires my love and support. Having someone so dependent on me and therefore having to put his needs first is a whole new area of practice but at the same time is actually always there regardless of whether you have a child or not. We are all reflections of each other and there are many moments in our days that require us to get over our selves. That's universal.*

You are here

That's enough of other people. Let's come back to you and to now.

The most important moment in the history of mindfulness is now. I don't mean that in some kind of wishy-washy spiritual way, I mean that completely literally. People talk about the mindfulness movement as if it is some kind of abstract idea; it is not. All the mindfulness movement is is people like you doing whatever they can to make their lives that little bit better. It is what is happening right now as you read this paragraph. Strip back all the hype, the newspaper inches and the research papers and what we have is just you, just here. The simple fact that you have got to this point means that you have a genuine interest in this stuff. Recognise that. Acknowledge that.

Realise that just reading this book is itself a way of you taking care of yourself. Appreciate that.

Those of us who take care of ourselves from the inside out not only make a real difference to themselves but also to the world around them. So your reading this book to this point is also an act of generosity to others. Notice how that feels.

Yes, you will struggle to remember to do the various exercises. Yes, there will be times when you won't be fully sure if you're doing a particular technique properly or not. Yes, you will sometimes find it impossible to find even two minutes for some formal practice. Yes, there will be some times when it all gets too much and mindfulness is the last thing on your mind. That's OK. That is just what being a twenty-first-century meditator is like. I know.

At the start of this book I introduced three ways in which this approach to mindfulness was a bit different. Firstly it was mobile. So many people find it a real challenge to find quiet time for themselves and so to base our whole meditation practice on that diminishing resource is never

Those of us who take care of ourselves from the inside out not only make a real difference to themselves but also to the world around them.

going to work out. Therefore we just have to turn how we approach meditation on its head and learn how to embed it alongside the sixteen hours of the day we do have. There are then no more excuses for not having time, and all we need is to know what to do and remember to do it. Through trying out some of the six core techniques and sixty meditation exercises perhaps you've hopefully begun to get a sense of how effective, fun and sustainable that can be.

I also talked about meeting people where they are, letting them make their own way through mindfulness based on what their particular needs are at the time. That is the reason the book is structured like it is. Feel free to come back to individual chapters whenever you want. Take what you need, not only from this book but from the whole field of mindfulness and meditation. They were designed as practical tools to help people live life more fully and freely so do use them however feels right.

The third distinctive aspect to how mindfulness is presented here is in its relationship with technology. Our lives are now at the point where talking about virtual versus real, online versus offline, digital versus analogue is becoming anachronistic. It feels clunky to talk about our 'digital lives' since they are just our lives.

So that's my work done and what happens now is up to you. Like it or not, how you use your attention and awareness trains how you are, how you think and how you behave, and how you are, how you think and how you behave affects the world around you. So there are ultimately just two simple questions. What do you want your mind to get better at? And what is the world you want to build? There have been lots of ideas, techniques and stories shared in these pages but now it's over to you and your story.

There are a lot of different routes you can take from here. You might have enjoyed the book and think that mindfulness is a nice idea but leave it at that, perhaps coming back to it as an actual practice later on in life. Or you might start giving it a go, mainly using the techniques and ideas at times of real need. Or you could start trying some of the exercises whenever you remember them and enjoy the benefits which come from that. Or you might really take it on, deepening your interest through the combination of mobile and formal practice so that over time meditation becomes a core part of your life. You may even develop enough momentum so that awareness, calm and kindness become your natural and spontaneous way of being. That would be nice.

All of these outcomes are fine. There is no one-size-fits-all approach and it is for us to find our own way through.

It has been an absolute pleasure to write this book. Not only has it been a delight to share some of what I've learnt from my own adventures in mindfulness, but the very act of writing a book about constant mindfulness has helped brighten my mind and sharpen my practice. There is a beautiful old tradition from way back, where at the end of a long meditation retreat, the leaders of the retreat ask forgiveness of those who have taken part. So as one final connection from the very old to the very new, I would like to do the same. Should there have been anything in this book which you've found difficult to understand, any references which have been too obscure, any jokes too unfunny, then I ask for your forgiveness.

I wish you all the best with wherever you go from here.

This is happening.

Further Reading and Watching

Sayadaw U Tejaniya on naturalising mindfulness
Awareness Alone is Not Enough

Kelly McGonigal on the value of embracing the difficult
The Upside of Stress

Sharon Salzberg on trusting your experience
Faith

George Mumford on applying mindfulness to elite performance
The Mindful Athlete

Jane McGonigal on the power of playfulness
Reality is Broken

Chogyum Trungpa on the dangers of confusing spirituality
with self-improvement
Cutting through Spiritual Materialism

Natasha Dow Schüll on understanding how software traps our attention
Addicted by Design

Alex Soojung-Kim Pang on improving our relationship with our devices
The Distraction Addiction

Clay Shirky on Information Overload vs Filter Failure
https://www.youtube.com/watch?v=LabqeJEOQyI

Nathan Jurgenson on digital dualism and fetishising 'real life'
http://thenewinquiry.com/essays/the-irl-fetish/

Rohan & his work

The Person
rohangunatillake.com

The Company
mindfulnesseverywhere.io

The Apps
buddhify.com
sleepfulnessapp.com

Acknowledgements

Gratitude is a lovely thing and that this book exists at all is down to two people. The first is my friend and agent Julia Kingsford who told me I had to write a book and as with everything else she was absolutely right. The second is Carole Tonkinson who took a chance on me and whose experience, insight and wider team have been invaluable.

Given that mindfulness has been a part of my life for so long and I'm no teacher in any conventional sense, I don't always have a good sense of what is most useful for people starting out on their own adventures to know. Xaki Barnett, Emmie McKay and Andy Young have all been brilliant at telling me what worked and what didn't as the words started to stitch themselves together. Suzy Glass and Ed Howker also in their own ways made this book better than it might otherwise have been.

Almost five years ago I decided to make a meditation app. I primarily made it for my friends who wanted to try mindfulness but felt they didn't have the time. I never imagined that this side project that went on to become buddhify would not only be used by so many people around the world but would become the basis for my whole work life. The fact that I can describe myself as a meditation entrepreneur will always feel somewhat ridiculous but I am very fortunate to be in this position. I am therefore deeply grateful to everyone who decided to make buddhify and our other products part of their lives. Thank you especially to those of you who write in with your stories of the difference they have made. Your words make all the hard work so worthwhile.

In my years of practice I have had the outrageous fortune of having many wonderful teachers. I have trained with and been influenced by a wide range of people but there are ten who stand out the most. Ajahn Sumedho for holding tradition and innovation at the same time. Ajahn Vimalo for showing me the value of humour. Sayadaw U Tejaniya for encouraging me to be playful. Christina Feldman for being such a boss. Sharon Salzberg for reminding me the heart comes first. Jack Kornfield for helping me with the importance of exploring different practice styles. Rob Burbea for pointing me to the deep stuff and giving me the confidence to walk there. Martin Aylward for balancing the ordinary and the extraordinary. Kenneth Folk for his pioneering energy and Bhante Kovida for suggesting I give meditation a go in the first place. You are the best.

Everyone who agreed to talk to me and share their stories and experiences for the book has been incredibly generous. Thank you to Jennifer, Chris Dancy, Kirsten Schultz, Amy, Patrick, Chris O'Sullivan, Andres Roberts, Louise Chester and Michael Bready. Extra special thanks to my friends and heroes Emily and Vincent Horn, whose work with Buddhist Geeks has been so important to me.

Finally, I am deeply grateful to my family for their support and love, even when they might not be quite sure of what I am doing. Most of all, thank you to my wife Lucy for telling me to cut out the jokes. The book is much better for your wisdom, as indeed am I.

About the Author

Rohan Gunatillake studied at Oxford before beginning a career as a management consultant. One day he realised the hustle and bustle of his morning commute could actually enhance his meditation rather than prevent it and his concept of mobile mindfulness was born. Rohan combines twelve years' experience of working in technology and innovation with an equally extensive background in mindfulness, and through his company Mindfulness Everywhere makes a range of creative and human-centred products which combine meditation, technology and design including buddhify, which has been a bestselling app in over forty countries. With his emphasis on playfulness and digital culture, Rohan is recognised as one of the most creative yet authentic voices in modern mindfulness; he is a trustee of the British Council and in 2012 *Wired* named him in their Smart List of fifty people who will change the world. Rohan and his family live in Glasgow.